D1257348

IN DEFENSE OF RELIGIOUS LIBERTY

AMERICAN IDEALS AND INSTITUTIONS SERIES

Robert P. George, series editor

Published in partnership with the James Madison Program in American Ideals and Institutions at Princeton University, this series is dedicated to the exploration of enduring questions of political thought and constitutional law; to the promotion of the canon of the Western intellectual tradition as it nourishes and informs contemporary politics; and to the application of foundational Western principles to modern social problems.

In Defense of Religious Liberty

David Novak

Wilmington, Delaware

Copyright © 2009 ISI Books

All rights reserved. No part of this publication may be reproduced or transmitted in any form or by any means, electronic or mechanical, including photocopy, or any information storage and retrieval system now known or to be invented, without permission in writing from the publisher, except by a reviewer who wishes to quote brief passages in connection with a review written for inclusion in a magazine, newspaper, or broadcast.

Novak, David, 1941-
In defense of religious liberty / David Novak. — 1st ed. —
Wilmington, Del. : ISI Books, c2009.

p. ; cm.
(American ideals and institutions series)
ISBN: 978-1-933859-75-0 (cloth) ; 978-1-933859-76-7 (pbk.)

Includes bibliographical references and index.
1. Freedom of religion. 2. Church and state. 3. Natural law.
I. Title. II. Series.

BV741 .N68   2009 2008928731
323.442—dc22   0901

ISI Books
Intercollegiate Studies Institute
Post Office Box 4431
Wilmington, DE 19807-0431
www.isibooks.org

Manufactured in the United States of America

to Robert P. George

Contents

Preface

To speak of religious liberty is to speak of three surprisingly different things.

First, one can speak of the liberty one gains from being part of a religious community and its tradition. That liberty consists in the way that God, whom the religious community looks to as its beginning and its end, liberates the members of the community from that subjection to the world and death which is everyone's worldly fate. This world and all who are of it will surely pass away. And so this first kind of religious liberty is exercised apart from the world; it can only be experienced within the holy times and places when and where the community celebrates its intimate relationship with God.

Second, one can speak of the liberty one's religious community claims from the world. This kind of liberty consists in the religious community's freedom from subordination to the political powers that be, and it usually means the freedom to practice the rituals of worship without political interference. Here, religious liberty is exercised against the world, since the secular world often looks jealously upon any political autonomy exercised by religious communities.

Third, one can speak of religious liberty as the freedom of a religious community to bring its own moral wisdom into the world, especially the moral wisdom it regards as available to everyone precisely because that wisdom can be presented with cogency by means of worldly reason. This kind of religious liberty is exercised for the world, even though many in the world may resist it, presuming that it is only a ploy covering a socially or culturally imperialist agenda.

The religious liberty discussed in this book is of the third kind. I do not deal with either the existential liberty that comes from one's communal relationship with God or with the political liberty religious communities claim from their respective worldly societies. Rather, I intend to show how the adherents of a religious tradition—in my case, the Jewish tradition of which I am part and to whose teaching I am committed—can represent the moral wisdom of their tradition in a way that avoids the extremes of imperialism on the one hand and obsequiousness on the other. In a certain way, I am responding to the question asked by the Jews in Babylonian exile: "How do we sing the Lord's song on strange ground?" (Psalms 137:4). Clearly, experience has taught us that we cannot sing that song in the same way we would sing it on *holy* ground. On the other hand, I argue in these pages that we ought not and cannot change the song altogether; in the terms of our metaphor, we must simply sing the Lord's song in a different octave. We must cogently bespeak the moral wisdom of our faith traditions, and that means affirming that those traditions are about much more than the world—much more, but nothing less.

With the exception of chapter 5 ("God and Human Rights: A Biblical-Talmudic Perspective"), all the chapters in this book began as lectures given to various audiences in different places. Furthermore, readers can get a better idea of the specific content of the individual chapters by looking at the detailed table of contents.

I hold both U.S. citizenship (from birth) and Canadian citizenship (by adoption). Some people might charge that this reflects a fatal ambivalence, but for me worshiping one God, and adherence to one religious tradition, is "monotheism" enough. When it comes to worldly societies, I am a "pluralist." I would never give up the privilege of U.S. citizenship, because I was born a U.S. citizen. But I am also a Canadian citizen; that is the country where I now live and work, and to which I want to make a contribution as a full member of society. Moreover, the great issues of public morality dealt with in this book are almost always identical in both countries.

Chapter 1, "Religious Liberty as a Political Claim," began as the first of the three Charles E. Test, M.D., Distinguished Visiting Scholar Lectures I was honored to give at Princeton University in the fall of 2004. Specifically, these lectures were given under the aegis of the James Madison Program in American Ideals and Institutions, a program in which I am honored to be a consulting scholar and a member of its board of directors since its inception. Additionally, I was a William E. Simon Fellow in the program in the spring semester of 2006. The fact that this excellent program is part of Princeton's politics department, and the fact that the Madison Program is made up almost entirely of religious people very much involved in the political/moral expression of religious liberty, made the reason for choosing this topic for my opening Test lecture obvious. For the wonderful hospitality, cooperation, and sympathy of Dr. Bradford Wilson, associate director, and Judith Rivkin, then events coordinator, I express my gratitude here.

Chapter 2, "Religious Liberty as a Philosophical Claim," began as the second of my Test lectures. This lecture was a challenge, since its philosophical tone has a certain Kantian quality, whereas the general philosophical trend of the James Madison Program is often more Thomistic. Clearly, on almost all questions of public practice, there is virtual unanimity among the scholars associated with the program; yet at the more theoretical level there are some big differences. This can be seen when examining all the Test lectures (and other lectures) given here-tofore under the Madison imprimatur. The fact that this lecture received such an attentive and respectful hearing testifies to the genuine intellectual pluralism at work in this academic commu-nity. Another version of part of this chapter was delivered as a lecture, "Human Rights as Divine Entitlements," at the twenty-fifth anniversary celebration and conference of the Center for the Study of Law and Religion at Emory University in Atlanta on October 26, 2007. I am grateful to center director John Witte Jr. for the invitation to deliver this lecture on that auspicious occa-sion, and for his encouragement of my work over the years.

Chapter 3, "Religious Liberty as a Theological Claim," began as the third and last of my Test lectures, delivered on November 22, 2004. This lecture, where my Judaism is most evident and explicit, deals with how claims for their religious liberty in non-Jewish societies have been made by adherents of the Jewish tra-dition, but also how the Jewish tradition has enabled its adher-ents to exercise liberty in various ways throughout its history. This lecture was meant to belie the notion that a commitment to a religious tradition and a commitment to religious liberty are a hopeless paradox, if not overt hypocrisy.

Chapter 4, "Religious Liberty in a Secular Society," began as a lecture delivered to a largely Evangelical Christian audience at Trinity Western University in Langley, British Columbia, on June 6, 2002, as part of a conference titled "Keeping the Faith." This conference was called largely in response to the attempt in British Columbia to prevent teachers graduated from Trin-ity Western from teaching in public schools, because their reli-gious tradition considers homosexual practices to be immoral. As part of the response to this threat, which could come from my own religious tradition just as easily as it comes from theirs, I attempted to bring some insights from my own worldly experi-ences and reflections. I am grateful for the encouraging response to my lecture from the faculty, students, and friends of Trinity Western who were present on that beautiful June day.

Chapter 5, "God and Human Rights: A Biblical-Talmudic Perspective," is a slightly rewritten version of a chapter of the same title in the volume *Does Human Rights Need God?*, edited by Elizabeth M. Bucar and Barbra Barnett, and published in 2005 by the William B. Eerdmans Publishing Company. (I thank Eerdmans for permitting me to republish this essay in this volume.) At a time when many secularist enemies of religion in public life have argued for the impermissibility of using the name *God* (the *G* word) in public discourse, I was especially happy to be asked to write this essay by my friend Jean Bethke Elshtain of the University of Chicago, a scholar and thinker who has shown how one can speak of God in public discourse, and without being easily dismissed by those who would like to be more selective (or prejudiced) as to whom and what to admit to or reject from that discourse.

Chapter 6, "The Human Rights of the 'Other' in Jewish Tradition," began as a lecture delivered at a conference on "The Human Other," under the auspices of the Catholic Faculty of Theology in Lugano, Switzerland, on September 19, 2005. An Italian translation of the original lecture was published in *Annuario Direcom* (2006). I am grateful to Father Libero Gerosa of the Catholic Faculty of Theology, and his assistant, Dr. Elke Freitag, for the invitation to deliver this lecture to a truly international audience, and for their hospitality during my stay in Lugano. I also benefited from conversations with my two other Jewish presenters at this conference, Shimon Shetreet of the Hebrew University of Jerusalem, and Asher Maoz of Tel Aviv University. It was especially significant in this context to be working with these two distinguished Israeli legal scholars, who demonstrated in their presentations how seriously the State of Israel takes the ancient Jewish tradition of concern for and protection of the strangers in its midst, a tradition I could only describe by quoting and explicating classical Jewish sources.

Chapter 7, "Law: Religious or Secular?," is a slightly revised version of the Meador Lecture on Law and Religion, which I delivered at the University of Virginia Law School on October 14, 1999. It was subsequently published as an article of the same title in the *Virginia Law Review*. (Thanks to the editors of this respected journal for allowing me to republish this essay here.) The original suggestion of this invitation came from my late lamented University of Virginia colleague and friend Nathan A. Scott Jr., who was quite instrumental in bringing me to the university's Department of Religious Studies in 1989 (where I served as the first Edgar M. Bronfman Professor of Modern Judaic Studies until January 1997). I was often thinking of Nathan when revising this lecture and article, because I have tried to emulate what he did for literature—by showing its inescapably religious character—by trying to show the same is true for law.

The invitation to write this book, as a written version of my Test lectures at Princeton along with some other related essays, came from the Intercollegiate Studies Institute (ISI), and I thank Jeremy Beer and his staff for the invitation, for their insightful editing of my manuscript, and for shepherding this book through the publication process. It is a better book because of their efforts.

I first started revising and rewriting these lectures and articles when I was visiting professor of religion in Princeton's celebrated religion department during the spring semester of 2006. During that happy time, I enjoyed and learned much from colleagues and friends there, especially Leora Batnitzky, John Gager, Eric Gregory, Martha Himmelfarb, and Peter Schäfer. They and other colleagues and students made that semester a delight. And I could not have spent that semester without the kind permission of the Faculty of Arts and Science of the University of Toronto and its then dean Pekka Sinervo. Also, my thanks go to Dr. Matthew LaGrone (now teaching at the University of Delaware), my former doctoral student and research assistant, for his efforts in preparing the index and bibliography, and for his fine command of English prose that he used so well in helping me make my own writing more intelligible.

The mention above of Princeton provides me with a good segue into the dedication of this book, to my very good friend and close colleague, Robert P. George, the McCormick Professor of Jurisprudence at Princeton and the director of the James Madison Program in American Ideals and Institutions there. "Robby" (as he is called by just about everybody with whom he works) and I first met at a conference at Princeton in 1986, almost immediately after he arrived there to teach as a freshly minted Oxford D.Phil. We were actually brought together at the suggestion of John Finnis, Robby's Oxford "Doktorvater," who is the close collaborator of my Georgetown "Doktorvater," Germain Grisez. We hit it off instantly, and we have been working and talking together ever since. What Robby does for his friends is well known far beyond the circle of his friends. This is a way for one of those friends to express his gratitude. May God grant him many more years of life and strength to be a champion (among other good causes) of genuine religious liberty in the world.

Toronto, Ontario
Erev Rosh Hashanah 5769
September 2008

Part One

1

Religious Liberty as a Political Claim

Religious Liberty and the American Story

Religious liberty is something largely taken for granted by most of us who live in constitutional democracies. After all, who could deny that liberty? Is there someone in a position of political authority stopping any of us from worshiping or not worshiping wherever, however, and for whatever reason we please? More particularly, isn't the founding cultural story of the United States of America celebrated by the one holiday Americans actually founded: Thanksgiving Day? Every November, Americans once again celebrate how, in 1621 at Plymouth Rock, their "pilgrim fathers" (and mothers, sons, and daughters) first celebrated the right to worship according to their conscience, according to what they believed to be their sacred duty. Indeed, it was for that right perhaps even more than for their having been saved as a community from starvation (despite the loss of many individuals) that the pilgrims truly did give thanks. By so doing, they have inspired a nation to do likewise with their families every year.[1]

Perhaps this is why the United States has no such similar national celebration of the earlier settlement of the country by Englishmen, namely, the Jamestown settlement of Virginia in

1607. That might well be because these earlier settlers came here for purposes of conquest, enrichment, exploitation, and enslavement, purposes so much less exalted and less inspiring than the quest for religious liberty.[2] Indeed, the story of Jamestown could have just as easily been the story of Spanish or French colonization of the New World. But what happened at Plymouth Rock was qualitatively different from the other settlements of North America, even those of fellow Englishmen whose primary interests were certainly not religious.

The American story as it is now told is very much the story of English North America. That becomes quite evident when we look at the whole question of religious liberty. As for earlier settlements of America by Spaniards and Frenchmen—the Spaniards were conquered by English-speaking settlers by the middle of the nineteenth century; and the French were, in effect, sold to English-speaking settlers by Napoleon in the Louisiana Purchase of 1803. Thus they too, like the conquering English-speaking settlers before them, had to become attuned to a notion of religious liberty their earlier national identities had by no means prepared them for.

Most other subsequent immigrants to American shores have come for cultural reasons remarkably similar to those of the pilgrims. Even African Americans, the one major group of Americans brought here forcibly in chains as slaves, had to see their story as a pilgrim-like tale of liberation from slavery (both political and spiritual) on the way to redemption. That had to be their story, with all its biblical overtones, in order for African Americans to become willing participants in the American story. No one in recent times made that point better than Martin Luther King. Thus we have seen the adoption of an essentially English story, even though those adopting it have not had to become white, Anglo-Saxon, or Protestant in the process.

By their very perilous move to what, for them as Europeans, was indeed a strange, savage, and most uncertain land, the pilgrims were exercising their religious liberty in a way that indicated, to use more modern language, a truly existential commitment. More specifically, they were thanking God for getting them out from under the ecclesiastical clutches of an established state religion—the Church of England—from whom they had separated. But let it be remembered that the pilgrims had left England after a short, experimental sojourn in the Netherlands. It was there they decided to risk being English Calvinists in a far-off English colony rather than becoming Dutch Calvinists in a land where they would have to make a political break with their past by becoming citizens of a foreign polity.[3] In the Netherlands, they would also have had to make a break with their cultural past by seeing their children quickly adopt Dutch as their new mother tongue. Politically, the pilgrims wanted to remain loyal to the British crown, though that was also the "crown" worn by the very same king who was the head of the very same church from which they had separated in order to form their own religious community. (Unlike the Mennonites, for example, they had no problem recognizing the moral legitimacy of the earthly state and participating therein.) The pilgrims very much wanted to remain the English Protestants they had been for almost a century.

In their own time, the pilgrims were called "separatists," unlike the more numerous and more powerful "Puritans" of Massachusetts Bay Colony, who never officially separated from the Church of England, but who only wanted to reform it. (In that sense, the Puritan political vision was remarkably similar to, if not actually copied from, John Calvin's theological-political state in Geneva a century before.)[4] Moreover, these same Puritans were most anxious to establish their own religious domination in the New World, something the pilgrims consciously eschewed. The pilgrims, followed by Roger Williams in Rhode Island, who himself had separated from the theocracy (clerisy being the more accurate name for it) of the Massachusetts Bay Colony, set a strong precedent for the idea that religious allegiance does not preclude allegiance to the state any more than allegiance to the state must subsume the religious allegiances of each and every citizen and therefore dictate them.[5]

In seventeenth-century America, the most the pilgrims of Plymouth Colony (which was eventually subsumed into Massachusetts Bay Colony in 1691) could do was to try to forge for themselves a status of religious exceptionalism, like those who, after 1688 in England, came to have the status of "dissenters." In other words, they did not ask for the disestablishment of a state church, only that they not be required to pay allegiance to that state church. Nevertheless, the pilgrims did set the stage for the eventual separation of church and state that came with the first amendment to the Constitution—the so-called "nonestablishment clause"—almost a century and a half after the Puritan settlement in the Boston area. For most Americans, this separation of church and state lies at the core of what we mean by religious liberty. Thus, if the state in any of its institutions is not telling us what to do or not do when it comes to religion, we are safe in our religious liberty.

Despite all this, though, many Americans feel threatened in their religious liberty. There are those who feel threatened by the so-called "Religious Right," believing that its political power is designed to force upon them a religion they do not want. And there are those who consider themselves religious—"right," "left," or "center" politically and economically—who feel threatened by forces in society that regard any public religion to be inimical to authentic democracy. (Some have named the ideology of these forces "secular humanism.") But if there is to be genuine political discourse in our society, we need to be able to rationally present our own political view vis-à-vis religious liberty and defend it from the more irrational charges of its opponents: whether that be the charge of a religious coup d'état or the charge of a secularist coup de grâce.

This process of public reasoning must begin with some initial clarification of what we mean by religion, that is, what Richard John Neuhaus has called "religion in the public square."[6] Accordingly, we need to clarify what we mean by religious liberty. Since almost everyone would agree that the question of religious liberty is important, both for society and the individual, we should try to clear up some of this confusion by proposing conceptual definitions—however tentative—for these key terms, and then show how they suggest, if not actually propose, certain basic political positions. Neutrality toward the available political options regarding religious liberty is not itself an option for any responsible citizen inasmuch as one cannot hide from a question that stalks the citizenry at every significant turn. In fact, writing around the time the pilgrims settled in America (albeit in Latin and in the Netherlands), Spinoza devoted perhaps his most enduring work to this the "theological-political" question—which is still very much the larger question of democratic society as it was the question of the nation-states in the seventeenth century.[7] The question of the separation of church and state is only a subset of that larger theological-political question, a larger question that is no doubt perennial.

Not being a lawyer, much less a constitutional scholar, I will not pursue the complicated politics and jurisprudence of religious liberty in general, and church-state separation in particular, in the United States (or in any other polity for that matter—like Canada, where I now live and work).[8] Furthermore, despite the fact that I am a scholar of Jewish law and theology, I cannot have any expert opinion on the question of church-state relations even in the Jewish state of Israel, for Israel is not civilly governed by Jewish law, and it does not see its mandate to be coming from Jewish theology even in principle.

I would now like to discuss what I, as a nonspecialist in American law and politics, think religious liberty means, and how that meaning affects politics, philosophy, and theology in a constitutional democracy like America's—and beyond. I can only claim some expertise in the areas of theology and philosophy, but not in the area of secular law and politics. Yet it is with the political question I wish to begin, since the most immedi-

ate location of the question of religious liberty is in the realm
of politics. The historical point made above was only made to
show how the question of religious liberty is ubiquitous in the
American story from the very beginning, and how religion and
politics have been continually intertwined with each other in
that story.

Rights and Liberties

Since we have seen that religious liberty is so central to the
American story, let us examine now what we mean by religious
liberty and how it affects life today.

Most people would see "liberty" to be synonymous with "having a right." But what does it mean to have a right? I would define
a right to be a justified claim of one person upon another person
or persons.[9] Making the claim itself is the exercise of a legally
recognized right. Liberty, though, is not so much a claim itself
as it is what is being claimed. When I claim religious liberty for
myself from other persons, especially from the state as a corporate person, I am claiming two things or one of two things.
Minimally, I am claiming noninterference in the practice of the
religion of my choice—what Isaiah Berlin called "negative liberty."[10] (But this negative liberty is not the same as what Louis
D. Brandeis called "the right to be let alone." Liberty is much
more than a lone, individual matter.)[11] Maximally, I am claiming assistance in the practice of the religion of my choice—what
Berlin called "positive liberty."[12] In the case of negative liberty,
the state's duty is one of passive restraint; in the case of positive
liberty, the state's duty is one of active support.

Most people, I think, would settle for religious liberty in the
negative sense, fearing that the active support of religion by
the state could easily turn into the imposition of the religion of
those having the most political power over everyone else. For
those having little or no political power, that possibility raises
the specter of religious coercion: what the pilgrims feared from

the Church of England. But even those who share the religion of the politically powerful need also worry that the possible imposition of that religion on their fellow citizens will inevitably corrupt that religion, causing others to despise it—maybe even causing themselves to despise it as well. Nevertheless, there are times when people do have to seek some active support from the state for the sake of their religious liberty, and they should do so.

Regarding negative liberty, the noninterference one seeks must also be a claim for all those who want to practice their own religion, that is, liberty for religion (for *religions*), as well as liberty from religion, that is, liberty from the imposition of any religion either by the state or any private person or group. Without my willingness to make a claim to my own religious liberty for everyone in general, whether that be to practice a religion or not to practice one, my own claim for myself alone smacks of special pleading. At most, making myself an exception to a general rule rather than being an instance for the application of a general rule, that would be a plea for tolerance. Yet is that not tantamount to presenting my way of life as being so irrelevant to the life of civil society itself that the state need not be bothered with interfering in it? But that could only be the case if my religion, as well as the religions of others, made no public moral claims upon me or upon society itself—that is, if religion were simply the practice of some arcane, maybe even quaint, rituals. So, my claim to religious liberty should be ordinary, not extraordinary (a point to which I shall return later).

The fact is, every religion makes moral claims upon its adherents. Moreover, every religion that affirms the universality of human nature also insists that there are moral claims upon all the members of any wider society in which there are a multiplicity of religions and nonreligion. Morality, whether specific or general, is a system of claims and counterclaims: one claims as a person; one is claimed by other persons. Morality manifests itself as the systematic correlation of rights and duties. Since religion has such a powerful moral presence, the state must either respect or disrespect the moral claims of the religions in its midst. The call for respect or disrespect indicates relations far more intense than those indicated by tolerance or intolerance. One can ignore someone whose eccentricity is tolerated; one cannot, however, ignore phenomena like historical religions whose very phenomenality is so morally laden. And, as Aristotle best argued, ethics and politics are two sides of the same coin.[13] Humans are by their very nature ethical-political beings. All morality, as Alasdair MacIntyre has perceptively argued, is unintelligible outside a real political context.[14]

When there is genuine social respect for the religions that members of society have chosen to be part of, we then have true "multiculturalism." When the term is properly understood, it is anything but a cover for the type of cultural relativism that leads straight to moral nihilism. Authentic multiculturalism is when a variety of cultures conclude that they hold certain moral norms in common just as much as they conclude that they hold certain other moral norms separately, that is, not in common.[15] The norms the various cultures do hold in common are already so generally prevalent that we can assume, indeed insist, that the burden of proof be on those who would deny them, not on those who have been traditionally upholding them. To be sure, these general norms only comprise part of the overall normative teaching of any culture and, in fact, not even the most important part of that normative teaching. Yet it is the only part of that normative teaching that is able to make claims on a society wider than the borders of the cultural community itself. Thus Maimonides, the great twelfth-century Jewish jurist, theologian, and philosopher, stated about the prohibition of shedding innocent blood, which is certainly the chief example of this multicultural moral commonality: "Even though there are iniquities more serious than bloodshed, they do not entail the destruction of civilization [*yishuvo shel olam*] like bloodshed. Even idolatry, and it goes without saying: forbidden sexual relations [*arayot*] and Sabbath desecration are not like bloodshed."[16] In other words, greater generality does not mean greater importance at the level of the transcendent horizon of any culture, what Maimonides, following the Talmud, terms "what is between humans and God."[17] Nevertheless, greater generality does make for greater importance at the interhuman or political level of human existence. This is because what has greater generality has more evident intelligibility to all rational persons; and because, in fact, such general norms are constantly in operation in all those cultures where human personhood is respected and valued.

I might add that much of what today is called spirituality—that is, metaphysical-type meditation outside the context of religious traditions—seems to be so attractive to otherwise secular people because it makes no moral claims on those who engage in it. But, along these lines, could one imagine anything like the clash between King Henry II of England and the Archbishop of Canterbury, Thomas Becket, for example, if Becket were only engaging in private spirituality rather than engaging in very public moral admonition of his fellow Christians and the state itself in matters of elementary justice? King Henry probably would have thought that such "spirituality" would happily keep Becket out of political mischief. But Becket was not martyred because he was "spiritual"—in the current sense of the term anyway.[18]

Ethical Community

When we are dealing with religious liberty, we are dealing with religion. And when we are dealing with public religion, which it seems is the only religion that can bear the name coherently, we have culture. In many ways religion and culture is a language, one that comprises both words and deeds. Its morality comprises the main part of what we could call its active grammar. As Wittgenstein pointed out so accurately, there is no such thing as a private language.[19] Language, being communication between communicators, necessarily takes place outside any proverbial "closet," as the philosopher Jürgen Habermas has shown so well.[20] As Aristotle pointed out long ago, language is a political phenomenon in the same way politics is a linguistic phenomenon.[21] Thus language as an essentially political medium is always morally laden, even when moral demands are not always its explicit content. Multiculturalism is best represented when it shows that there are some areas where the moral grammar of different cultures overlap. Nevertheless, that overlapping (a favorite term of the philosopher John Rawls), although not accidental, is still not truly universal.[22] In the political sphere, it enables religious coalitions, as it were, to make some general claims upon the body politic. The question of ethical universality, which is more than just generality, must wait for a philosophical investigation of religious liberty (the subject of chapter 3).

I would define "culture" as the substance of the life of a historical community, those normative practices that give the particular community its identity in the world and that bind the members of that community to each other both contemporaneously and intergenerationally. Moreover, these cultures inevitably see themselves against a transcendent horizon, that is, they are concerned with how they are an integral part of the cosmos: the universal order. At this level, we are dealing with religion, even if, as is the case with Buddhism, the ultimate cosmic principle is not a personal God. At the level of the interhuman, such a community is what Kant called an "ethical community."[23] At the level of the divine-human relationship, such a community is what Jews call *keneset yisrael* ("the congregation of Israel"), what Christians call the *ekklēsia* ("the Church"), and what Muslims call the *umma* ("the people"). Clearly, these three respective designations of religious cultures refer to much more than a mere aggregate of historically developed institutions. Each of them has a significance that is transcendent, or what some would call "mystical."

The interchangeability of culture and religion, religion and culture, comes out in the very etymology of the English word *culture.* Most scholars see the root of the Latin *cultura* to be *colere*, which means "to cultivate." One can cultivate a place in the sense of inhabiting it with others. That is its ethical meaning. One can also cultivate or attend to the objects of religious concern: *cultus.* That is its cultic or religious meaning.[24] Every culture—that is, the way of life of a historically continuous people—has had its cult, with its religious practices and the God whom they attend. Thus, when one deals with the question of culture, one cannot avoid the God question. But how the question of God is addressed in the political discourse of a secular polity is no simple matter. Members of religious communities cannot expect a public answer to the God question that is a simple "yes," and secularists cannot expect a public answer to that same question that is a simple "no." In a democratic polity such as ours, claims to religious liberty are made by and for the sake of an ethical community. A secular polity is in a position to cogently judge the political validity of the ethical claims made upon it and whether it is to respond to them or not. But a secular polity is in no position to judge the validity of strictly religious claims other than to see them as part and parcel of the internal cultural life of an ethical community. Thus, a secular polity is in no position to judge the validity of the revelation transmitted by any ethical community as its founding event, nor the special religious claims that revelation makes upon the members of that ethical community. Accordingly, religious liberty is quite different from what is usually seen to be "freedom of thought," which turns out to be some sort of individual preference: a private right or right to privacy.

Religious liberty is the claim a historically continuous ethical community makes upon a secular polity. The claim to religious liberty is a public claim made to elicit a public response. Almost all private rights (with the exception of the right to individual life) are entitlements from society that can be easily taken away, it is hoped with good cause, of course. Think, for example, of how easily one's right to private property is taken away whenever the state transfers wealth through the exercise of its power of taxation. The most we can hope for is that this right of the state is not exercised capriciously, that it is exercised by truly authorized persons, and that it is directed with clear vision toward the common good. But our whole democratic tradition seems to regard the right to religious liberty to be more than an entitlement, at least more than a human entitlement. Thus tying this religious right—this right to religion, and even the right to be free from religion—to notions of privacy, let alone thinking that privacy has some sort of absolute priority over the public realm (however conceived), is both confused in its logic and unable to find any true precedents in fact. No one today has pointed this out better than Judge Robert Bork, especially in his criticism of recent U.S. Supreme Court decisions that confuse permissions of privacy from the state with rights that are truly prior to the state, both historically and ontologically.[25]

Ethical Claims

Whereas the right to religious liberty was usually beyond dispute in the past, at present it is under attack when it comes to the ethical claims traditional religious communities have been making upon the state, and especially the ethical claims these communities make in matters of sexuality and the definition of what constitutes a family in American society. For most people, notions of what is their family and what is their cultural community are inextricably bound up with each other. This is becoming apparent, primarily, in the great public debate on the question of same-sex marriage, a question that now seems to have overtaken the debate on abortion in popular attention. Like the debate on abortion, the debate on same-sex marriage is largely a debate between religious people and secularists, even though some religious people are in favor of same-sex marriage and some secularists are opposed to it. Nevertheless, the religious people who are in favor of same-sex marriage are hard pressed to show how such a radical innovation can be justified by the sources of their own tradition. And secularists who are opposed to same-sex marriage are equally hard pressed to show that their opposition is not based on mere nostalgia, or on their opposition to marriage altogether, that is, same-sex couples should not be afforded civil marriage because no one should be afforded civil marriage.

In fact, though, the opposition to the secular recognition of same-sex unions as marriages has come almost exclusively from religious quarters. Hence many of the proponents of same-sex marriage have argued that limiting marriage to heterosexual couples—as has been international, multicultural practice until recently—is a form of religious coercion, even though that limitation is certainly not being advocated by any one particular religious tradition to the exclusion of all others.[26] That raises the whole question of whether morality, for most people anyway, is derived from religion or not. We shall examine that question quite extensively in the next chapter on religious liberty and philosophy. But now it is sufficient to say that religious coercion is only contrary to the Constitution when it is the establishment of one religion as the moral arbiter of society. And by religion here I mean a culture that is grounded in an event of divine revelation in history, one whose content is then transmitted and developed (*traditio*) throughout history, and one that is finally completed at the end of history (the *eschaton*). However, it is not "religious" coercion, it seems to me, when there is a moral consensus among a variety of religious traditions (and even seemingly nonreligious traditions like English Common Law) on any particular question of public practice like marriage.

When proponents of same-sex marriage complain about the imposition of the "Judeo-Christian religion" on society, they are complaining about a phantom of their own imagination. The fact is that there is no such thing as the Judeo-Christian religion; instead, there are two religions: Judaism is one religion; Christianity is another religion.

Now these two religions, essentially different as they indeed are, have certain things in common. For many, the most important thing Judaism and Christianity have in common is an almost identical list of basic moral norms. So, it is correct to speak of a "Judeo-Christian morality."[27] Nevertheless, this is not a morality that Jews and Christians made up together. Rather, it is a common morality that Jews and Christians accepted separately and then discovered that their respective acceptances are virtually identical because they were made for many of the same reasons. That is especially the case as regards the sanctity of human life and the sanctity of marriage as an institution for a man and a woman to form a permanent union for the primary, but not exclusive, purpose of begetting and raising children. Moreover, although Christianity received its sexual morality through Judaism, around the year 1000, European (and later even non-European) Jews accepted the Christian definition of marriage as being monogamous: one man and one woman.[28] (The exact reasons for that initial acceptance, however, are still quite obscure. But I would like to think that Jews accepted that Christian definition of monogamous marriage as being true to the spirit if not the exact letter of Judaism itself.)

In the public debate over same-sex marriage, religious people need not only defend themselves from the charge that they are imposing their religion on society at large, but they must also see the movement for same-sex marriage to be an assault on their religious liberty. That is because of the way the movement for same-sex marriage has made its own case.

Since same-sex marriage was not allowed by any civil jurisdiction until quite recently, proponents of same-sex marriage have had to argue that the previous exclusion of homosexual couples from the institution of marriage has been a form of unjust discrimination. This exclusion from the public institution of marriage has been compared to the now-illegal practice of denying African Americans access to public educational facilities. But what about religious communities who deny homosexual couples the sacrament or covenant of marriage? Furthermore, the clergy of these religious communities, in the United States and Canada (and in many other democracies), also function as de facto civil servants since they are required to be licensed by the state to perform marriage ceremonies.

In fact, the practice of most clergy today is that they refuse to celebrate the wedding of any couple who have not first obtained a civil marriage license. (It is also standard rabbinical practice to require a civil divorce decree in hand from a couple seeking a religious divorce before proceeding with the religious dissolution of their marriage, known as a *get*.) Nevertheless, some clergy have faced civil penalties, for example, for having not required a civil marriage license from widows and widowers whom they have united in a second marriage. It seems these couples only wanted a religious ceremony for their second marriages, but one not registered with the state, because they did not want to lose their Social Security benefits from their first marriages. As far as the state is concerned, they wanted to be unmarried widows and widowers; but they did not want to be "living in sin" when it came to the law of God as taught by their religious community. (Apparently, defrauding the state did not raise their moral hackles as the possibility of "living together" surely did.) But wouldn't there be a similar probability of civil penalties for couples living in jurisdictions where same-sex marriages are already civilly recognized if these same couples only wanted a religious ceremony? Couldn't the clergy who celebrated these "religious-only" marriages be subject to civil penalties as well?

Many religious people would not want to participate in the institution of civil marriage if that institution included same-sex unions, for to do so would be giving tacit approval to the state's legitimatizing—even "blessing"—sexual unions that are morally odious to most religious people. That is much more than religious people tolerating the refusal of the state to interfere in the private sexual relations of consenting adults. Marrying is a public act requiring public approval in order to be valid. Involvement in civil marriage, whether as a participant or a celebrant, entails one's endorsement of the institution itself and thus the marriages of all its other participants as well. It is like voting in an election. When I cast my ballot, I thereby endorse the right of every other voter to vote as well.

Despite the probability of civil penalties, though, I know of several Protestant clergymen in Ontario (the province where I have lived since December 1996), where same-sex marriage is now legally recognized, who have publicly announced that they will no longer sign civil marriage documents, and that they will only officiate at weddings that conform to their religious law. Signing civil documents that attest to what is now accepted as "marriage" in Ontario violates their religiously formed conscience, hence they cannot do so in good faith. But how can these clergy as de facto civil servants refuse homosexual couples the wedding ceremony when it has become in some places their civil right? Aren't these clergy unjustly (that is, arbitrarily and prejudicially) discriminating against a class of persons, namely, homosexuals? To avoid this kind of charge that could be made against a cleric as a de facto civil official, a few clergymen have removed their names from the provincial registry of licensed marriage officiants altogether.

To assuage the fears of religious people that their clergy might be forced to celebrate same-sex weddings, thereby blessing same-sex marriages, two suggestions have been recently floated.

First, it is suggested that when the statute defining marriage as an essentially heterosexual union is changed, clergy of those religious communities who do not recognize same-sex marriages will be exempted from any obligation to celebrate weddings of same-sex couples in the same way they are not required to celebrate weddings of couples who are not permitted to marry according to their own religious law. So, for example, an orthodox rabbi will not be subject to civil prosecution if he refuses to celebrate the wedding of two homosexuals in the same way he is not subject to civil prosecution when he refuses to celebrate the marriage of a Jew and a non-Jew. Another example would be a Catholic priest who refuses to celebrate a same-sex wedding in the same way he refuses to celebrate a wedding between two civilly divorced persons. In such cases, the rabbi or the priest would be exercising his right to religious liberty. Wouldn't it be difficult to force a clergyman to perform a religious ritual he could not in good conscience perform?

Two, it is suggested, more radically, that the state simply get out of the "marriage business" altogether. That is, instead of providing domestic partnerships as some jurisdictions (like Vermont, for example) now do for the minority of couples (all of whom seem to be homosexual) who cannot marry under present marriage law, the state should simply establish an institution of "domestic partnership" and leave marriage, in effect, to religious communities and their own adherents. It is argued that this is what has been the case in France for over a century, namely, citizens first register their marriages civilly and then, if they so choose, they can get a religious ceremony from whatever religious community will celebrate their union as a marriage. (It is interesting, though, that at present France does not recognize same-sex marriages and does not seem likely to do so anytime in the near future.)

Both of these suggestions, however, still constitute an assault on religious liberty, especially in the ethical claims religious communities make upon the state, for the following reasons.

To claim an exemption from accepted public practice has been the tactic employed by what are usually called "sectarian" religious groups. Groups like the Amish or the Hasidim ask to be exempted from many public practices on the grounds of their right to religious liberty, in their case the right to communal liberty, that is, to be a quasi-independent polity. The hidden premise of their arguments is not one that can be made as an explicit legal argument in a democratic context, for a secular democracy cannot recognize the political jurisdiction of religious bodies.

But this hidden premise can be explicated in a more informal social context. The premise is these religious "sectarians" are only partial members of the society, even if they are legally citizens of the state, that they regard themselves to be foreigners and want others to recognize them as foreigners too—that is, when it suits their own sectarian interests.[29] The state frequently complies with these claims to exemption because these groups are regarded as being so bizarre and so numerically insignificant that, for pragmatic reasons, it is simply not worth the bother of forcing them to be participants in a political order that they really do not accept as being their own. Nevertheless, like all entitlements from the state, the right to be exceptional can easily be rescinded, for reasons equally pragmatic. Furthermore, such an entitlement is more likely either not to be given or more quickly rescinded when the religious bodies to whom it has been given are both numerically more significant and, most importantly, the members of these religious bodies very much regard themselves to be full participants in the political and social order. As such, they are neither marginal nor arcane foreigners: not in their own eyes, nor do they want to be in the eyes of their fellow citizens.

In Canada, where same-sex couples are now already allowed to partake of civil marriage, clergy of those religious bodies who do not sanction same-sex marriage have so far been exempted from having to officiate at same-sex weddings. And in the legislation that is to be presented to parliament, and upon which the Supreme Court of Canada will be asked for constitutional review, this exemption is explicit. But, as with other such entitled exemptions, which are clearly at odds with the egalitarian logic of the legislation itself, religious people have good reason to be wary. They are well advised by Scripture: "Do not place your trust in princes," thus they should be rightly suspicious of the tolerance of those in political power "in whom there is no help" (Ps. 146:3).

In fact, religious people don't have to imagine what could easily happen. It is already being publicly announced. Thus some political leaders in Québec, the Canadian province where religion was once strongest in the nation and where it now seems to be the weakest, have stated that they will not necessarily be bound by any exemptions stipulated in the new national marriage act for Canada. In other words, they will comply with the logic of the new marriage act more consistently than the politicians in English Canada are willing to do—so far. And even though religion has been in steep decline in Québec for the past two decades, whatever religion is left there is still overwhelmingly Roman Catholic. It is very unlikely that the Québecois politicians, almost all of whom are either lapsed or minimally practicing Catholics, will essentially "tolerate," that is, ignore, their present or former church by letting its opposition to the new law of the land go unchallenged. Surely they do not look upon *l'église catholique* to be an insignificant sect they need only tolerate. It is clear that they fear whatever moral force the Church still has in their society and will, no doubt, act to cripple it. Furthermore, even were there to be such tolerance, it would be both ephemeral and essentially degrading to religious people, who are not at all prepared to go into exile from a society upon which they have at least as much of a claim as the militant secularists who would have them treated as foreigners there. I can't imagine the political situation would be all that different in the United States. Think of Massachusetts with its large Catholic population, but whose supreme court has nonetheless recently authorized the registry of same-sex unions as marriages thus making Catholic marriages, in effect, civilly exceptional. And this civil exception is also the case with Evangelical, Eastern Orthodox, and traditional Jewish marriages there, and anywhere else in the world where same-sex marriages are recognized by civil law.

As for the suggestion that the state get out of the marriage business altogether, that clearly implies the whole institution of civil marriage has been a mistake. Thus, rather than radically redefine it to a point where it loses any essential continuity with the way marriage has been understood in the past, those suggesting this are arguing that we should act as if the venerable institution of traditional (actually, intertraditional) marriage, which the state has heretofore recognized by its institution of civil marriage, should now be looked at as if it never existed at all. It is like the annulment of a particular marriage: it never was, even retroactively, since it never should have been when viewed retrospectively. Yet this too infringes on religious liberty. And that is because this suggestion does not understand very well how civil marriage came to be and why it provides an important benefit to the polity, that is, why it well serves the interest of the state, which is the common good.

In the seventeenth century, civil marriage arose in England, primarily to provide the civil benefits of marriage to persons who were not members of any traditional religious community, either due to their own choice or due to the choice of religious communities to exclude them from membership. (Civil marriage also arose as a result of Oliver Cromwell's attempt to remove the monopoly on marriage held by the Church of England.)[30] Nevertheless, civil marriage was not set up to replace traditional religious marriage, the type of marriage it was assumed most citizens would still obtain for themselves. In fact, civil marriage largely imitated religious marriage, especially in its adoption of the theretofore exclusively religious requirement of marital faithfulness and, therefore, its adoption of the religious requirement that there be culpability for adultery. And, because these moral obligations may not be overruled, even by the mutual consent of the marriage partners (think of what is still called "open marriage"), that means civil marriage resembles a religious covenant more than it resembles a civil contract—so far, that is. For this reason, it seems, religious people have been willing to accept civil marriage as a social institution, and they have been willing to civilly register their own marriages with the state accordingly.

Marriage and Children

This acceptance of and participation in civil marriage by religious people indicates that they have approved of the reason the state takes an interest in marriage per se. The secular reason for the state's interest in marriage is that children are conceived through the sexual union of a woman and a man, and that children are best brought to birth and reared when that union is an ongoing process rather than a random event. The state has a clear interest in the conception, birth, and effective nurturing to adulthood of its future citizens. That secular reason for the state's interest in marriage as we have known it heretofore is quite consistent with the religious reason for marriage. It is why religious communities promote marriage. The secular reason is consistent with the divine mandate: "Be fruitful and multiply" (Gen. 9:1); "Take wives and give birth to sons and daughters" (Jer. 29:6)—which is because God "has formed the earth to be a dwelling" (Isa. 45:18), that is, we truly inhabit the earth when we make our intergenerational home in it.[31] Indeed, the secular state can advocate the immanent reason for that divine mandate, even though it cannot celebrate the transcendent source of that mandate.

Children are best raised by the permanent union of the woman and the man responsible for their physical origin in the world, that is, those who conceived them in the first place. In fact, if you don't believe me on this point, please consult some children, especially those whose parents have divorced or who were never married and separated, and ask them what they think the optimal family situation for themselves and all others like them ought to be. Aren't their claims on the parent or parents who abandoned them justifiable? So, religious people can well recognize that all children, even those whose parents for whatever reason do not want to be part of any religious community or cannot be part of any religious community, deserve to have their own family kept intact. Thus the state still has the duty to institutionalize the kind of marriage that is most likely to conceive children and raise them to maturity. To date, that is a heterosexual union primarily designed to be procreative. It is thus the duty of the state to privilege this institution of marriage for the sake of the children who usually emerge from it.

The duty of the state to protect the traditional institution of marriage is in direct response to the right to life of every child conceived, and to the right of every child born to have an intact family. All children have that right despite the fact that—alas—more and more children in our society cannot exercise that right anymore because their natural parents refuse to respond to that right dutifully. All the more so, then, does the state have the duty to support and not dilute the institution of traditional marriage by generalizing it to the point where it could include any human relationship imaginable. The state should do so for the sake of every child born and growing up in its midst. Yet the state today, in many cases, is doing less and less to enforce these rights of every child, a point usually missed by advocates of what now goes by the name of "children's rights."

I might add, this argument in favor of the rights of natural children and their natural parents in no way rejects the state-created institution of child adoption, that is, when parents are either unable or unwilling to raise their own children to maturity. Under these circumstances, these children are certainly better off being raised by people who want to care for them and to do what is in the children's best interest. The state is obliged to facilitate this new relationship in loco parentis. Nevertheless, the burden of proof is on the natural parents to show why they are unfit to parent the children they have conceived and brought to birth. Minimally, that means the identity of both natural parents be registered with the state. Thus, along these lines, I could make a moral case against the state's permission of anonymous sperm donors and anonymous surrogate mothers. Maximally—and this is quite debatable—adopted children have a right to know who conceived them and brought them to birth. Yet prudence would also dictate, if we go this far, that this is the only claim adopted children have on their natural parents. They may not demand that their natural parents take them back, as it were, because the adoptive parents who are raising them, by virtue of that fact, have a claim on the honor and respect of their adopted children.[32] They have earned that much by having rescued these children from the abandonment of an orphanage and giving them a home. And, finally, because these adoptive parents have rescued these children from orphanhood, they have the right to raise their children in their own religion (provided they have one, of course).[33] Here we have another example of religious liberty as a political claim on the state not to interfere in what religious parents would regard to be something their tradition requires of them, whether they are raising their own natural children or adopted children.[34]

Getting back to marriage, the state still does and should continue to institutionalize traditional marriage for the sake of the common good of society. Part of that common good is the sound mental health of as many citizens as possible. By every sociological indication, children growing up in homes where they are cared for by the same two people who conceived them in the beginning grow up to be happier and more productive citizens. This is not just a Judeo-Christian point. When Plato thought that the elite of his ideal polity would best be raised by the state itself, thus bypassing the traditional familial structure, his student Aristotle reminded us that those who grow up with no attachment to a natural family have no family-like attachment at all to extend to society as a whole.[35] In other words, eliminating the specificity of family life, best grounded in marriage as all our traditions, religious and secular, have basically known it, does not lead to a more general social commitment; rather, it leads to the emptiness of personal rootlessness in the world. As David Hume recognized, moral sentiments are centrifugal, extending from the more intimate to the less intimate; they are not centripetal, beginning with the more general and then deriving the more intimate therefrom.[36]

For this reason, then, religious people can regard civil marriage as being consistent with, or even enhancing of, their own sacramental or covenantal marriage. That can be seen as a positive liberty to be enforced by the state. And for this same reason, ministers of religion like myself can sign the civil marriage registry in good conscience, because we are genuinely happy to be assisting the state in its worthy institution of civil marriage—at least so far in most places in the United States and in the world at large today.

Now there are some religious people who have argued that if or when a state recognizes same-sex marriage, then their religious community should only celebrate religious wedding ceremonies and tell the couple that if they want civil marriage as well, they must obtain it on their own. More radically, these clergy should tell a couple that they will celebrate their wedding religiously only if the couple avoids civil marriage altogether. Of course, considering the fact that there is now solid data indicating that 35–40 percent of heterosexual couples in Canada who are living in "long-term relationships" are doing so without the blessing of either church or state, religious people opting out of civil marriage are hardly doing anything very daring. So, if those more radical in their view of marriage than even the proponents of same-sex marriage want to kill the institution of marriage as we know it, they should convince religious people to opt out of it as fast and as numerously as they can. When the deserters outnumber the troops, the army will have to shut down.

Yet, were that to happen, it might well be that exclusively religious marriage would become the only kind of marriage available in any recognizable sense of the term. In fact, this is the case today in Israel, where there never has been an institution of civil marriage. Along these lines, it is noteworthy that in Canada, where only 80 percent of the population profess belief in some deity—the percentage of those holding membership in a distinct community of God-worshipers being still less—still more than 90 percent of all civil marriages are celebrated under religious auspices. As such, it would seem that even otherwise secular people still see civil marriage as beholden to the earlier traditional-religious model. They prove that point by where and by whom they wish to be wed. So, I think it quite likely that were "marriage," however defined, to be replaced, not just supplemented, with a civil institution of "domestic partnership," that most Canadians would continue to opt for religious marriage, and that far fewer of them would even bother with registering as "domestic partners." Without the traditional term "marriage," a sexually centered relationship otherwise named has all the luster of a driver's license.

I am sure the proponents of same-sex marriage know this too, and that is why they want to be included in the institution of marriage, not to abolish it altogether. And they also know that were civil marriage itself to be abolished, the proponents of traditional heterosexual marriage have an earlier historical location in which to be married, whereas the proponents of same-sex marriage have no such place to turn for a blessing. Finally, speaking in terms of practical politics, since only 3 or 4 percent of the population is homosexual, and it is likely that far less than half of that percentage are even interested in the bonds of matrimony, the departure of even far less than the 90 percent of married couples in Canada from civil marriage would have far greater political consequences than including those same-sex couples who even want the institution of marriage at all.

Despite the scenario I have just imagined, there is no indication that the majority of the citizenry in either Canada or the United States want to change the definition of marriage. Therefore, it is a premature admission of defeat for religious people to assume that they have already lost their battle for religious liberty, which in this case means their multicultural understanding of the meaning of marriage. They need not yet become countercultural, then antisocial, and eventually outlaws. Accordingly, their vigorous legal and political defense of traditional marriage and family lies on the frontier of the defense of religious liberty in general.

That is the politics of religious liberty as I see it. Nevertheless, politics without adequate reflection on the intelligible foundations of praxis quickly turns into the type of ideology that can be reduced to sound bites. To prevent that, we need to examine religious liberty as a philosophical issue.

2

Religious Liberty as a Philosophical Claim

Morality and Religion

In the previous chapter on religious liberty and politics, we saw how the exercise of the right to religious liberty becomes publicly controversial when religious communities choose to make moral claims on the secular body politic. As for the cultic claims of these same communities, however, claims we would call strictly "religious," such as claims to practice singular forms of worship, these are rarely controversial in a secular society. Instead, the strictly religious controversies involving these cultic matters are almost always confined to the cultural space of the religious community; they can only be made on their own members. Any faithful Jew, Christian, or Muslim can readily attest to the frequency of intrareligious controversies over these internal claims, especially in an age when traditions have had to be defended more frequently by their own adherents even within their own communities.[1] That is why secular courts are loathe to adjudicate intrareligious disputes. Only when certain civil aspects of such disputes are so pronounced that the line between the sacred and the profane is very much elided would a secular judge be civilly irresponsible to recuse himself from a case involving a dispute within a religious community. Nevertheless, as we shall see in chapter 4, secular courts are already intruding in the right of religious communities to make moral claims on their own members.[2]

Religious communities have a much bigger problem in publicly advocating what they take to be universal norms. That is not only their *political* problem; even more, it is their *philosophical* problem. Thus, religious people must be prepared to answer this question: How does one advocate a public moral position identifiable with one's religious tradition in a society that does not look to any religious tradition for the justification of public morality? Surely, the political disestablishment of religion means that civil society may no longer look to any religious community for the authorization or justification of any public policy, let alone for any specific legal warrant.

How one justifies a public stance that is consistent with one's theology without invoking that theology as its public authorization is a philosophical question. It requires a philosophical answer. Unfortunately, though, when it comes to raising this question, much less answering it cogently, religious communities have not been too articulate, let alone persuasive. And I suspect that their political ineptitude is largely because of their lack of philosophical clarity on this and other public claims of religious liberty they make in public. So let me be so bold as to try to help religious communities make at least a more plausible, if not more compelling, philosophical case for their public moral claims. I do this, of course, with a vested interest in the matter, myself being an active member of one such religious community—a community that could and should be more vociferous in its advocacy of certain public norms, norms that are not simply for the sake of its own particular political interests.

The philosophical problem of religious advocacy in a democracy is based on the following question: Must religious people derive their public morality from their theology? Or, does morality need a religious justification in order to be valid? If the answer is yes, then while the personal motives for what religious people advocate can be based on theology, or anything else for that matter, they cannot expect their fellow citizens to accept moral positions based on these same personal motives. More publicly acceptable reasons are required if there is to be even the possibility of rational assent from persons whose theologies are different, and even more so from those who have no theology at all. Not only may civil society not require commitment to some theology on the part of its citizens, it may not even require any theological commitment at all from them. That is because theologies as we know them conceptualize historical revelations, and in the deepest sense we citizens of a multicultural democracy do not share a common history, a history that is a "history of salvation." We do not share a sacred history that extends from revelation to redemption, a history that gives us our true place in the order of the universe. That is why as citizens of a multicultural democracy, we are not a chosen people nor should we act as if we were.

In theological perspective, a certain community believes that God has spoken to them. They in turn have accepted that revelation as the foundation of their communal life, a revelation whose occurrence and whose content is then transmitted (*traditio*) to each succeeding generation. The interpretation of the historical narrative of revelation and the ongoing interpretation of its normative content is the task of theology. As for the tradition's normative content, theology is also needed to apply that content to new situations and even to considerably reformulate that content because of new situations. Narrative theology deals with the context of revelation; normative theology deals with the content of revelation. As such, theology speaks the language of historical authority, an authority that cannot claim prima facie rationality so as to make it compelling to the rest of the world that has not already included itself in a singular historical narrative and accepted its norms. (I say "singular" rather than "particular," since no faith community regards itself to be a "part" of a larger

whole called "religion," a whole that can be accessed by some
sort of induction.)

Faith, which connects adherents to their own religious traditions, cannot be taken as either a self-evident premise or a
necessary conclusion from self-evident premises. Faith is not
a form of philosophical reasoning. Philosophy can prepare one
for faith, even deepen it, but philosophy cannot automatically
engender faith. Faith is not so much a leap from the rational
into the superrational as it is one's acceptance of a communal
narrative by including oneself within the narrating community,
together with the confidence that its story is essentially true,
even if not verifiable by external criteria. There is no way of
ascertaining the truth religions teach without believing—that
is, accepting with certainty—the testimony of the persons who
have witnessed this truth and then transmitted it to their community. ("You are my witnesses, says the Lord" [Isa. 43:10].) Faith
is the way one accepts what the tradition has to say, how it be-
speaks the covenantal relationship with God (*brit*) given to the
members of the faith community by revelation and through its
historical transmission.[3] One's keeping the commandments is
his or her active expression of his or her practical fidelity to God,
the object of faith. "Faith" (*emunah*) is the objective confirmation of revealed truth (*emet*) about what God does in relation to
us and with us. "Trust" (*bitahon*) is the subjective confirmation
of the One who continually reveals his word to the faith community, and now to this individual believer.[4]

Neither faith nor trust is possible unless the faithful, trusting
believer is already within the communal narrative in order to
live according to its law. Thus, when Ruth converts to Judaism
under the guidance of her mother-in-law, Naomi, she first states
"your people are my people," and only then can she say "your
God is my God" (Ruth 1:16).[5] It is not that Ruth is accepting a
merely tribal deity; rather, she is accepting the universal God,
creator of heaven and earth and the creator of all humankind.
Yet Ruth's acceptance of that God is not universalizable; rather,

she has covenanted with God as God has uniquely covenanted with the people of Israel in their history. That is why Boaz blesses her in the name of "the Lord God of Israel under whose wings you have come for shelter" (Ruth 2:12). The actual universal acceptance of the universal God, though, will have to wait for the messianic future, the culmination of all earthly history, when, as the prophet says, "on that day the Lord shall be king over all the earth; on that day the Lord alone and his name alone" (Zech. 14:9).

That is what distinguishes theology and philosophy from one another. Theology is about history; philosophy is about nature. Theology is concerned with the truth of singular events in the world; philosophy is concerned with the truth of regular processes of the world.

Two questions now confront us. First, can one speak of God now in a way that could garner universal consent, especially universal moral consent? Can one speak of God in a morally plausible way, even when it is unlikely one will actually convince nonbelievers to either worship or obey that God? Can one speak of God philosophically, that is, from within any branch of philosophy?

Natural Theology and Natural Law

Since the term "nature" has always been contrasted with what is "conventional," the universal God has been called at times "nature's God." Is the cogent formulation of a natural theology possible, that is, a theology that can function independently of the historical theology of any singular faith community? Further, even if such a natural theology could be cogently formulated, could one ground universal moral norms in it just as faith communities have grounded their own moral norms in their own historical theologies? In other words, is "natural theology" philosophically plausible now as it was for many thinkers in the past? And was natural theology, even when it was more plausible than it is now, a sufficient source of public moral norms?[6] Since the terms "natural" and "universal" are often used interchangeably, I will use the terms "natural law" and "universal law" interchangeably too.

Natural theology assumes that there is evidence from the external world of a creator God who rules the universe in a lawlike manner. This natural theology has been stated most famously by Thomas Aquinas in his final argument for the existence of God:

> The fifth way is taken from the governance of things [*ex guberatione rerum*]. We see that things which lack knowledge, such as natural bodies, act for an end, and this is evident from their acting always, or nearly always, in the same way, so as to obtain the best result. Hence it is plain that they achieve their end, not fortuitously, but designedly [*ex intentione perveniunt ad finem*].[7]

However, do we really derive our sense of lawfulness, our sense of being commanded to do what is good, from what we have learned about the orderliness of the nonhuman world?

Even during Aquinas's time, when the reigning paradigm in natural science was a teleological one, when the finite universe was taken to be a good deal tidier than our messy, infinite universe, it was still quite a stretch to conclude from our experience of the external world that physical entities were being directed to their natural purposes by a superior power and intelligence. Even then, it was quite a stretch to conclude that the One God is in any way commanding all natural entities to move to their final destination.

In Aristotelian science, the science employed in Aquinas' day, natural ends are not designed into entities by an external and superior power and intelligence. Rather, natural ends are immanent within entities themselves. As such, they actualize themselves.[8] They are not "commanded" towards their natural ends in any way that suggests external, superior causality. Indeed, intersubjective causality, where one person commands or bids another person to do something, is always more impressive than natural causality: it exhibits a higher intelligence and a technologically more effective power than the "forces of nature." As such, we have to assume that we humans can improve upon natural material that is given to us rather than derive from that natural material a model upon which to direct our own lives. And let it be recalled that at the very beginnings of philosophy, Socrates explicitly argued that physics, even astrophysics, did not speak to him when he had to make moral choices.[9]

Since Galileo and Newton, we no longer employ a teleological paradigm in natural science, hence it is even more difficult to derive from nature anything like a view of causality that sees it as the action of a thinking, creative being, one whose superior creativity inspires us to formulate moral norms for ourselves in a process of *imitatio Dei*. As both quantum physicists and evolutionary biologists have taught us, nature's "creative" efforts are quite sloppy when compared with our own. Nature evidences more power than intelligence. Thus, what these scientists have taught us about nature hardly elicits worship, much less normative imitation. Indeed, in the biblical account of creation, humans are to "subdue the earth and rule it" (Gen. 1:28), and "to work it and to preserve it" (Gen. 2:15). But earthly nature is not to rule over humans.[10] As for the heavens, like the earth they are ruled by God, but we do not know how they are so ruled. That is why their nature is not a commanding paradigm, neither theoretically nor practically. "And from the signs of the heavens, do not be in awe" (Jer. 10:2). In fact, one of the greatest achievements of the religion of ancient Israel was to demystify and depersonalize both terrestrial and extraterrestrial reality.[11] In the biblical narrative, no nature, whether earthly or heavenly, was taken to be able to speak to us, much less command us or even mediate a commandment from God. Let it be recalled how God only answered Job that he governs the whole universe, but not how he governs it, let alone why he governs it the way he does. Thus in the Speech from the Whirlwind, Job is finally told by God: "Where were you when I established the earth? Pray tell if you know with any understanding [*binah*]! . . . Do you know the laws of heaven to locate its rule [*mistaro*] on earth? (Job 38:4, 33).

The theoretical as well as the practical problems of basing natural or universal law on natural theology are well appreciated by the contemporary Thomistic philosopher John Finnis, who writes:

> It is true that the natural law theory of, say, Aristotle and Aquinas goes along with a teleological conception of nature and in the case of Aquinas, with a theory of divine providence and eternal law. But what needs to be shown is that the conception of human good entertained by these theorists is dependent upon this wider framework. There is much to be said for the view that the order of dependence was precisely the opposite—that the teleological conception of nature was made plausible, indeed conceivable, by analogy with the introspectively luminous, self-evident structure of human well-being, practical reasoning, and human purposive action.[12]

So, whether one holds an immanent view of natural teleology, as does Aristotle, or a transcendent view of natural causality, as does Aquinas (largely influenced by Maimonides), neither view gives us a sufficient basis for the type of natural law philosophy that can be used to intelligently justify moral claims, such as the claim to religious liberty.

We need to be wary of natural theology attempting to be philosophy. Nevertheless, because of its venerable history and its use by the likes of Maimonides, Aquinas, and Calvin, certain natural law theorists today still quite uncritically make the highly tenuous connection between natural theology and natural law.

They still assume that natural law addresses its commands to human nature that is part of Nature as a whole. But it seems more sound, both philosophically and theologically, to assign the whole question of God's relation to the extrahuman cosmos to revealed theology, which tells us that there is an intelligent order operating in the cosmos, but an order that does not show itself to us directly, not even generally, let alone specifically.

A natural law case, especially a natural law claim for religious liberty, is better formulated without an appeal to natural theology. But can one cogently mention God in a natural law theory when natural theology, which constituted the chief element in premodern metaphysics, is no longer regarded as desirable, necessary, or even possible by most modern thinkers—and with good reason? So, must philosophers follow, for example, Hans Kelsen's philosophical rejection of natural law because it is essentially inseparable from by now philosophically discredited natural theology?[13] Or must theologians follow, for example, Karl Barth's theological rejection of natural law because it is essentially inseparable from theologically discredited natural theology?[14] The question, then, is whether or not one can connect God with an ethics that is based neither on natural nor on revealed theology. Can God be connected to a more philosophically compelling ethics today?

Natural Rights

Some see the modern idea of natural rights to be a complete break with the classical idea of natural law. As such, any similarity between the way classical natural law theory deals with God and the way modern natural rights theory deals with God, for them, is erroneous. Modern natural rights theory is taken to be essentially atheistic, implicitly if not explicitly. Thus, when modern natural rights theorists like Hobbes or Spinoza even mention God, it might well be a mere sop to their contemporary societies in which most of the people—and almost all the powerful people—were not only theists, but advocates of religions of revelation. So, when these modern natural rights theorists do speak of God, perhaps they are really winking at the few philosophers who can appreciate what they mean. One can see how this atheistic conclusion about modern natural rights theory was reached. If none of these modern natural rights theorists regards biblical law, with its commanding God, to be authoritative anymore, and if their invocation of natural theology is so uncritical, then it would seem that there is simply no other theistic alternative.[15]

I would like to argue that there is an alternative, that one can now connect God to a natural rights ethics without natural theology altogether, and aside from revelational theology for the time being. I attempt to do so by a radical reading of the most famous sentence in the Declaration of Independence, written by Thomas Jefferson in 1776. My reading is radical because I shall try to see meanings in this sentence that Jefferson himself would probably not have seen, but meanings that he nonetheless could not reject as contrary to his own intentions in principle. My reading of that sentence takes it to be a philosophical statement that admits of ongoing interpretation.

We all know the sentence by heart: "We hold these truths to be self-evident: that all men are created equal; that they are endowed by their Creator with certain unalienable rights; that among these are life, liberty, and the pursuit of happiness."

First, what is meant by a "self-evident" truth? Surely, the equality of all human beings is not self-evident. Wouldn't it be more self-evident to most people to say that all humans are not created equal? Humans are patently different: some younger and some older, some weaker and some stronger, some smarter and some dumber. And of course, we normally treat different humans differently. So, where do we treat all humans equally? Where is this self-evident equality to be found?

Nevertheless, the one sure place where the self-evident equality of humans is inherent is in the proceedings of a court of law, that is, in a court where the constitution of the polity of which it is a part mandates that the due process of law obtain. Here, doesn't every citizen have an equal claim to justice because every citizen is equally subject to the commands of the law and the protection of the law, the same law whose violation is being adjudicated in that court? That is why the due process of law is evidently contradicted if a court of law treats those standing before it for justice unequally. "You shall not pervert justice by privileging any person in judgment" (Deut. 16:19).[16] This is the best expression of the truth of the law not being "a respecter of persons."[17] So, taking a bribe to treat one litigant more favorably than the other is the prime example of such partiality, such unequal justice. That is why the prohibition of taking a bribe follows upon the more general prohibition of respecting persons in judgment in the norm just cited from the Bible, not as an example of biblical authority, but as a prime enunciation of this universally evident truth.

If persons are to be treated equally as litigants in a court of law where the due process of law obtains, and this is because they are all equally subject to the law by which they are being adjudicated, where does that prior law come from? Wherefrom are all these human beings commanded to practice the law by which they might be adjudicated should they be summoned as litigants in a civil or criminal trial?

If one says that this commanding source, this authoritative foundation, is the state, that begs the question, since one can then ask: What is the source of the state's authority? Why do I have to obey its commands? Why does this obligation make me subject to the adjudication of the state's courts if I am indicted for possible violation of those commands? Two answers are usually given to this overall question. One of them answers the question in a morally objectionable way; the other once again begs the question.

To answer that the state has prima facie authority is to assume that the power of the state need not justify itself. But if

that is the case, then the state cannot make moral claims on
our obedience because the state cannot justify those claims to
be rights. Moral claims must be justifiable or "rightful" (*iustum
est*) in order to elicit rational consent.[18] That consent is wholly
different from terrified surrender. Accordingly, in this case we
only obey the commands of the state because we fear its power
to harm us if we disobey those commands. Needless to say, this
approach makes any rational opposition to any kind of tyranny—whether of the ancient, medieval, or modern variety—impossible, especially if that tyranny has been codified into the
positive law of a tyrannically governed state. And in fact, it is no
accident that states who equate might with right—that is, their
might with what is right for everybody under their rule—frequently see themselves to be divine. They act in the political
realm according to Anselm's definition of the name "God" in the
ontological realm, namely, that which nothing greater can be
thought.[19] (And of course, if there is no higher ontological realm,
then the political realm takes its ultimate place by default.)

Even though the state is defined as a corporate person, in fact
the greater its power the more it needs to be governed by one
individual person. Thus the abstract divinization of the state
turns out to be the divinization of a real person. Think of the
cults devised by and for Hitler, Stalin, Mao Tse-tung, or Saddam
Hussein. Our rightful sense of horror at this prospect makes us
realize how the ancient prohibition of idolatry even precedes any
certainty on our part whether there is God or not. Even before
we have any certainty that there is God, we are keenly aware of
what is not God and what ought not be made into God. That was
a point, mutatis mutandis, made by both Paul in the New Testament and by the ancient rabbis in the Talmud.[20]

The usual way out of this idolatrous conundrum is to invoke
popular sovereignty, the type of sovereignty of the opening
words of the Constitution: "We the people of the United States
. . . do ordain and establish this constitution for the United States
of America." Yet that merely substitutes "the people" as autono-

mous subjects (plural) for the state as an autonomous subject (singular). But if that is the case, we hardly have the equality of which the Declaration so forcefully speaks. After all, if autonomy is power, even the power of intelligence, power is hardly distributed equally. So, where does the equality, especially the equality of rights, come from? Where is to be found the equality that the Declaration declares to be endemic to human nature, and of which our experience of the due process of law ever reminds us? Neither the autonomy of corporate power nor the autonomy of an aggregate of autonomous persons (Rousseau's "general will") can give us the equality that is so emphasized by our democratic traditions and our human experience of whatever justice is possible in this fallible world. So, it would seem that the Declaration deals with the question of law, while the Constitution only deals with the political procedures for administering that law and adjudicating according to it. But since these political procedures presuppose the law, the Declaration which speaks of "laws of nature" is the true preamble to the Constitution, logically speaking. Here I am giving philosophical expression to a historical point made by a venerable American historian, the late Avery Craven, in an unforgettable lecture I heard him deliver when I was an undergraduate at the University of Chicago, fifty years ago.[21] I do hope undergraduates nowadays still hear lectures that they will remember so vividly when they reach my age.

Divine Endowment

The Declaration speaks of "all men" being "endowed by their Creator with certain unalienable rights." But how is one "endowed" with a right? And, why is that endowment, though "self-evident," not self-referential? Why can these rights not be something the bearers of these rights by themselves give to themselves, neither collectively nor individually? In other words, why are these rights examples of heteronomy—understood to be a law from an other (from the Greek *heteros*)—rather than autonomy—understood to be a law from oneself (*autos*)?[22] Indeed, why do rights have to be given at all? Why can't rights be taken as innate?[23]

The reason one needs to look upon his or her rights as endowments rather than as innate properties is because of the persistent sense that we are commanded to pursue our rights and the rights of all others like ourselves.[24] Following our reading of the Declaration, that means that we feel commanded to pursue our rights, to make our claims to life, liberty, and the pursuit of happiness. Thus we are only able to intelligently exercise these rights, to intelligently make these justified claims, because we regard them to be commandments from our Creator. Indeed, we might say that God creates us humans uniquely by commanding us to pursue life, liberty, and happiness. And we shall eventually see how the pursuit of these three rights can best be taken as three instances of the exercise of one right, which is the right to practice one's religion. Furthermore, because I have been so commanded by God, I am empowered to make claims for my life, my liberty, and for the pursuit of my happiness. Since I experience these commandments to be categorical imperatives, these commandments pertain to any and all of God's free human creatures. They are universalizable: they pertain to anyone under the same general circumstances. As such, my pursuit of what I have been commanded must include my pursuit to help others keep these commandments as well. Like all such categorical imperatives, the subject of these commandments is "we," not "I." They are public, not private.

To illustrate how these commandments are received—how one is endowed with them—let me quote to you a powerful statement of how the first commandment, the commandment to live, was received in the most extreme circumstances possible: in Auschwitz, by a Polish prisoner there who wonderously—like all those survivors—lived afterwards, and who had enough presence of mind to write a deeply moving reflective memoir shortly after her liberation. Pelagia Lewinska writes:

> They had condemned us to die in our own filth. . . .
> They wished to abase us, to destroy our human dig-
> nity, to efface every vestige of humanity . . . to fill us
> with horror and contempt toward ourselves and our
> fellows. But from the instant I grasped the motivat-
> ing principle . . . it was as if I had been awakened
> from a dream. . . . I felt under orders to live. . . . And if
> I did die in Auschwitz, it would be as a human being,
> I would hold on to my dignity.[25]

Commenting on this cri de coeur, the Jewish philosopher
Emil Fackenheim (writing, I might add, about this non-Jewish
woman) asks: "She felt under orders to live. We ask: Whose orders? Why did she wish to obey? And—this above all—where
did she get the strength? . . . Once again 'will-power' and 'natural desire' are both inadequate. Once again, we have touched
an Ultimate."[26] In other words, "autonomy," be it the autonomy
of self-creation or the autonomy of raw instinct, is simply not
enough to explain the claim to live that was made on Pelagia
Lewinska, a claim to which she responded dutifully, and a claim
that her Nazi persecutors rejected hideously. Moreover, many of
us would like to believe that the crimes of these Nazi torturers
and murderers will be avenged by the divine Judge of the universe, the source of the very commandment Lewinska kept with
such difficulty and which these Nazi criminals violated with
such glee.

Lewinska hesitates to name the source of these orders "God"—
and who are we, Fackenheim reminds us, to tell her what to say.
But those who wish to pick up on her claim to life might be well
advised to make it in the name of God. That is the same God
who created her and us in his image and likeness, and who made
that unique creation known to us through our experience of being commanded to live at times in spite of our will and in spite of
our natural instincts. We are to live in spite of our will (and here
Fackenheim clearly has the Kantian autonomous will in mind),

since one's rational will could easily conclude that suicide is the only possible exercise of our autonomy under Auschwitz-like circumstances.[27] And we are to live in spite of our natural instincts (and here Fackenheim has something like Spinoza's *conatus* or Bergson's *élan vital* in mind), since from these instincts we could easily conclude that death is preferable to life under Auschwitz-like circumstances.[28] Perhaps this is what Freud meant by the *Todestrieb*, the "death drive."[29]

We can thus appreciate the insight of Karl Barth, who rejects Kant's avoidance of a truly transcendent source of moral law. Barth writes: "If there is an ought, it must not be the product of my own will, but touch from outside the whole area of what I can will of myself. . . . The essence of the idea of obligation is not that I demand something from myself but that, with all that I am demanding of myself, I am myself demanded."[30] Indeed, what Barth has exposed is the great paradox of Kantian ethics: How can I be both the source and the subject of the same act? Isn't the verb command a transitive verb? As such, how can the one who commands and the one who is commanded be the self-same person? And if one attempts to resolve this paradox by splitting the self into a higher "commanding self" and a lower "commanded self," then wouldn't it be better to see one's rational will (that higher self) as being obedient to the will of God who creates it through his commandments, commandments addressed to one's rational will?[31] Isn't a real, transcendent Other more authoritative than an immanent, imagined other? As Barth puts it: "Conscience is the totality of our self-consciousness in so far as it can receive and proclaim . . . the command of God as it comes to us. . . . The command is not revealed and given by conscience but to conscience."[32] That is what alone makes it a command. (I differ with Barth, though, by assuming that divine command can indeed be the authentic substance of natural law.)[33]

One needs to add the naming of God as the source of the commandment to live, and hence the right to live, lest Pelagia Lewinska's "feeling" be confused with some sort of blind impulse, the same sort of impulse that is claimed by the very criminals who felt impelled to torture her and kill others. By naming God as the source of both the commandment and the right to life, we turn our drive to live no matter what into a universal imperative from the creator of the universe who has given the earth to his human creatures that it might be a safe dwelling for all of us: to protect us from the violence of the natural world without and the violence of our own destructive impulses within. In other words, Lewinska's feeling, which was the immediate motivation of her active affirmation of her human life and dignity, is a justified claim, an authentic right, which enables her to claim that it be respected by all others. Minimally, her claim on other humans is that they not thwart her exercise of that commanded right. Maximally, her claim on them is to aid her in the fulfillment of this commandment to live. That is what essentially distinguishes a true right from the anti-universal, ultimately nihilistic claims of murderers and other criminals. These criminal claims have no justification that could be accepted by anyone other than the criminals themselves and their accomplices. Whatever "orders" these criminals feel compelled by could not be the commandments of the creator God since they attempt to destroy, not enhance, the created world. In the end, didn't Hitler kill himself when he ran out of victims?

This understanding of natural right, most immediately the natural right to life, does not require an acceptance of either revealed theology or natural theology to be a valid philosophical argument.

This understanding of natural right does not require an acceptance of anyone's revealed theology since there need be no historical paradigm in order for one to have an experience of being commanded by God to fulfill God's purpose in creating him or her or anyone else in the first place. In fact, such experiences have been reported by persons from a variety of religious traditions as well as by persons who do not consider themselves part of any religious tradition at all. And even when experienced

by persons from religious traditions, a self-evident truth has
been shown through that general experience. That is, the truth
presents itself here to be affirmed in action by those who have
so experienced it. It is not necessarily derived from any commandment written in anyone's Scripture, even if there is such
a commandment in someone's Scripture with which this self-
evident truth is wholly consistent. In fact, one could say that
such scriptural commandments themselves presuppose what
is experienced either before or outside of historical revelation.
Thus the commandment of the Decalogue "Thou shalt not murder" (Exod. 20:13) presupposes Cain's knowledge that killing his
brother Abel is wrong, and thus his knowledge of his responsibility for actually committing that crime. What the Decalogue
did, then, was to take an intuited precept, then indirectly regarded as if it came from God, and turn this precept into a commandment directly commanded by God himself.[34]

This understanding of natural right does not require an acceptance of what we have seen to be natural theology. That is
because it does not require a theoretical proof of the existence
of God and then the logical derivation of the practical reason
that constitutes natural rights from this proof of "nature's God."
So, in fact, following this line of thought about the Declaration
of Independence, we need to interpret Jefferson's invocation of
"nature's God" in a way that takes the term nature to refer to the
essential human condition—universal and immutable—and not
refer to the universe as a larger, encompassing whole. But if we
take nature here to be what it probably meant to Jefferson, the
connection between nature and natural rights as the rights of
man lacks any compelling logical connection.

Making this break with the view that Nature is a whole of
which we are but a part (a view best put forth by Spinoza), one
which Kant so thoroughly demolished in *The Critique of Pure
Reason*, we can employ Kant's logic here in taking the existence
of God to be a postulate of pure practical reason. Theoretical
or scientific reason cannot tell us anything about God or God's

relations to the nonhuman world, nor can it tell us how human praxis fits into that larger world. We can employ Kant's logic even though his postulation of God is inadequate to the name God, which minimally denotes "that which nothing greater can be conceived." For Kant, the God he postulates serves as the redeemer of human action, but human action whose ground remains human autonomy.[35] Even though God alone can make human moral action truly and fully effective, nonetheless, in the end, Kant's postulated God is subordinate to the ultimate project of human reason, just as a means is subordinate to its end. Kant's postulated redeemer of human moral impotence is not the Creator in whose image and likeness humans are made. It is not the God whose commandments to live, to exercise liberty, and to pursue happiness give us our true human identity in the world. So, I shall follow Kant's logic by analogy, but as a theologian I cannot in good faith accept either the premises or the conclusion his logic employs. But then again, practical or moral reasoning itself does not require one to be a Kantian when constituting its substance as a philosopher either. My epistemology is heavily Kantian, but my ontology and my ethics are definitely non-Kantian.

About postulates of pure practical reason, Kant writes: "These postulates are not theoretical dogmas but presuppositions from a necessarily practical point of view; hence, although they do not expand theoretical cognition, they do give objective reality to the ideas of speculative reason in general (by means of reference to the practical. . . ."[36] Now, something that is not demonstrable has no independent truth value. At most, it offers a more plausible explanation of the efficacy of moral law than competing explanations of that efficacy. Yet there is no proof of the separate existence of that divine cause. God is not what Kant would consider to be a direct object of experience of the external world or what can be employed to rationally explain that worldly experience. Postulating God in this way is always tentative and never fully conclusive. In our case, presuming—that is, postulating—God's general commandment to be the source of moral law, out of which natural rights emerge, seems to be a more satisfying explanation of moral obligation than postulating human autonomy as the ground of that obligation, which is what Kant does. Indeed, Kant errs in thinking that the ground or source of moral obligation can be directly intuited in human autonomy and thus itself be more than a postulate. Human autonomy is as much of a postulate as the existence of God, even for practical or moral reason. Moreover, I think it more plausible to postulate—that is, to presume—that God is the source of moral law than to presume humans are autonomous in any truly foundational way. Since neither of these presumptions can be independently proved, it would seem that the more plausible presumption should recommend itself to us over its nearest philosophical rivals, which are collective autonomy or individual autonomy.

Postulating God as the best source of natural rights does not make a judgment on whether or not God "exists" independently of our moral experience. Thus such moral postulation of God's existence cannot answer the question of whether or not humans can have a direct relationship with God in some other sphere of human experience and activity. Yet it might seem that if one leaves the question of God's existence at the level of morality, merely functioning as a postulate or practical hypothesis, one is bound to regard it as functioning like a legal fiction. And, as we know from legal history, legal fictions (*fictio iuris*) are tentative and easily replaceable with some other fiction, closer to the current popular imagination. Thus, when discussing natural rights as divine law (as did Jefferson in the Declaration of Independence), Alan Dershowitz writes: "It is one thing to say that natural law is a useful, even essential, legal fiction. It is quite another thing to say it actually exists. . . . The reality is that natural law simply does not exist, no matter how much we 'need' it or wish it existed."[37]

Here of course, Dershowitz is far less sober than was Kant, who knew he couldn't prove the nonexistence of the reality represented by an idea any more than he could prove its existence.[38] Moreover, one could certainly argue with Dershowitz's assertion that we no longer have a moral need for God as the source of human rights.[39] Nevertheless, if morality can only postulate God, rather than represent God as does theology (basing itself on God's word), then it is quite likely that those for whom this idea is their only relation to God (as distinct from a personal relationship with God) will tire of this hypothetical relation, moving to either a theological relationship with God or an antitheological stance against God. All this notwithstanding, though, even those who do have a theological relationship with God ought to avoid any futile attempt to derive rational morality from theological premises. Morality only implies religious reality; it does not necessitate it.

Unalienability

Finally, how are natural rights "unalienable"? If one postulates that these rights come from God through God's commandments to all humans to live, to be free, and to seek happiness as the ultimate good, then "the Lord giveth and the Lord taketh away" (Job 1:21). That is, these endowed rights, these divine entitlements, can be taken away from us by their divine Giver, and our experience tells us how they are in fact taken away from us all the time. As far as God is concerned, considering what we do know about God from biblical revelation, these human rights are most definitely alienable. God kills us by sending death; God removes our liberty by making some of us mentally incompetent; God prevents our attainment of happiness when he condemns some of us to oblivion in this world or in the world to come. In other words, God's judgment trumps any claims we might have on him for life, liberty, and the pursuit of happiness.

As commandments, the pursuit of life, liberty, and happiness are surely alienated when God takes away our ability to fulfill them. Instead, they are only unalienable in relation to the other humans upon whom we claim either not to interfere with our commanded pursuits or to actually help us pursue them. Now, of course, the unalienable character of rights is itself a claim and not a fact. It is an "ought," not an "is." We all know too well that other humans can and do take away our possibility to pursue life, liberty, and happiness. Surely, Pelagia Lewinska's persecutors almost removed her right to life as, indeed, they did remove her right to liberty while she was their prisoner; and for all we know they made her pursuit of happiness impossible even after her liberation from the death camp—at least in this world. Nevertheless, we do have a persistent claim on others for life, liberty, and happiness, a claim we certainly do not have on God. As a right (but not as a fact), these other humans cannot take it away from us. Furthermore, when they do take it away from us, we then have a claim against them. In a society where the due process of law obtains, we can claim—or others can claim on our behalf when we cannot make claims for ourselves—that the crimes that did alienate us from our life, our liberty, and our pursuit of happiness be avenged either by the payment of the criminal's property (restitution), the loss of the criminal's liberty (imprisonment), or even the loss of the criminal's life (capital punishment).

Life, Liberty, and Happiness

We have seen how one pursues life by feeling commanded to do so by higher authority ("under orders" in Pelagia Lewinska's memorable words) and how one's being so commanded is how he or she then exercises the right to pursue life as a claim upon one's society and its government. Or as in Lewinska's case, it is her right to resist the counterclaim of those governing her for her to actively cooperate in their program of killing her, first spiritually and ultimately physically. But, understanding the right to life to be the right to pursue life requires a slight emendation of Jefferson's own words in the Declaration of Independence. It will be recalled that we have rights to "life, liberty, and the pursuit of happiness." But I think that when we ponder just what the right to life means (and it is more than just a slogan used by those who oppose abortion), we realize that the right to life is the right to pursue life, especially to pursue life as something to be actively furthered and not just as something to be passively accepted as already granted. The same is true, as we shall see shortly, with liberty. So I would reinterpret Jefferson's sentence to say: the pursuit of life, liberty, and happiness. These pursuits, then, are "unalienable rights," which only God may ever take away from me, but never man—except on those rare occurrences when I grossly abuse them.

When it comes to the pursuit of life, we must see this pursuit as entailing the pursuit of communal life, which is endemic to our human nature. The first community we seek is our family, not so much as the family we already have, but the family we desire to found, to establish, in marriage. And that pursuit of marriage as the foundation of family, as a norm and not just as a fact, is itself the pursuit of life when its prime, although not exclusive, purpose is the procreation and rearing of new human life. Furthermore, this pursuit of the procreation of life is not just the fulfillment of the biological urge for genetic reproduction; it is even more so the moral choice to further our communal identity into a new generation. As such, this pursuit is the fulfillment of a commandment, which then leads to the exercise of a right or claim on those having political power over us. Once again, it is a minimal claim of noninterference in the fulfillment of this commandment by the government; and it is a maximal claim for active political and legal support of our pursuit of a fully communal and familial life.[40]

An example of how this right to life is pursued is the case of two friends of mine, an old couple now, who married and quickly had children immediately upon their liberation in 1945 from the Bergen-Belsen death camp. Why did they desire to marry immediately upon their liberation from the Nazi terror? As the husband put it in his typically straightforward manner: "It was not because we had to fulfill our sexual urges now that we were not starving." (In the near moral anarchy of the period immediately after the war in occupied Germany, there was no lack of opportunities for casual sex.) He said, "It was because we had to tell ourselves and tell the world that we were alive not dead, that we were going to rebuild our Jewish family, and that we were going to survive into the future by having Jewish children." In other words, my friends wanted to live and not just survive, and that meant they wanted to live as Jews in a Jewish family extending itself into the future by having Jewish children. (I can assume that other survivors, Poles like Pelagia Lewinska, felt much the same way; hence this imperative is not peculiarly Jewish.)[41] And, not being religiously observant or even very knowledgeable of traditional Jewish teaching at the time, my two friends, who became the husband and wife and then the parents they so wanted to be, actually learned this commandment from their experience of being incarcerated in a death camp and then liberated from it just before the persecutors could kill them as planned. I don't think they originally consulted the Torah. The commandment they desired to perform then became a right they exercised by claiming permission to civilly marry from the British Occupation Force, who then had political authority over them as displaced persons who were "stateless" at the time.

Furthermore, to continue our example, my two friends, who were not religiously observant but not atheists either, decided that they wanted a rabbi to officiate at their wedding ceremony. By so doing, they were pursuing liberty, specifically their right to freely (that is, with liberty) practice a religion into whose community they were now including themselves, however minimally at the time. That desire for rabbinical celebration of their marriage followed from their desire for a fully human communal and familial life. If they had chosen to have only a civil ceremony, which was possible, then they would not have been following the commandment they felt to live as Jews. The initiation of their marriage would not have had a Jewish stamp on it, and that could have very well led them to have no Jewish content in the home they planned for themselves in Canada, where they immigrated in 1949 (after four miserable, but still not life threatening, years in a displaced persons camp in Germany). In the cultural sense as well as the political sense, they still would have been stateless, they still would have been homeless in the world had they not sought out the rabbi for their wedding.

At last we come to "the pursuit of happiness." When we believe we are endowed by our Creator with the right to pursue happiness, just what sort of "happiness" are we being commanded to pursue? Before we can exercise our right to pursue happiness, which is our claim upon our government to let us pursue happiness and for that government to support that pursuit, we need to understand what it is we are claiming. If happiness means whatever we happen to regard as a good to be pursued, then what is being pursued might well be as multifarious as the number of people in such hot pursuit. Such happiness could be almost anything, that is, as long as its exercise doesn't harm others or threaten others with harm. Usually, society does not interfere with one's pursuit of his or her desire, that is, within the limits of one's respecting the rights of other people with whom he or she has to live in society. But if almost any pursuit is what is meant by "the pursuit of happiness," can one also insist with any cogency that this right is "unalienable," that it is a prior personal claim on society and its government rather than being a very much revocable or alienable entitlement from the state?

Could one claim, for example, one's happiness in owning a gun to be an unalienable, prior right, whose ontological or natural priority is something the state is duty bound to respect? Of course, there are people who do make such a claim, but that usually leads them to treat the second amendment of the U.S. Constitution (especially its second clause, "the right of the people to keep and bear Arms") as if it were divine revelation. But that is something both religious people and secularists would vociferously deny. Gun ownership may certainly be curtailed in the interest of the common good when, for example, unrestricted gun ownership increases opportunities for domestic terrorism. And if my point about gun ownership jars some of my friends on the political "right," I could just as easily jar some of my friends on the political "left" by seeing misplaced "unalienability" when they insist that the right to privacy, including the right to unrestricted sex between consenting adults, is some sort of natural right when, in fact, it is only an entitlement from the state. Sex between consenting adults may certainly be curtailed when, for example, one of the partners is HIV-positive, even if the other partner doesn't care about his chances of contracting the disease. In both cases, the state can rescind its entitlement of these permissions, either partially or even totally, when the state—either through the legislature or the courts—judges such permissions to be contrary to the common good of society. In other words, no one enters the social contract with such rights already in hand. In philosophical language, they are a posteriori not a priori, both logically and chronologically.

In fact, the pursuit of happiness is too precious to be rightfully exercised for anything less than the pursuit of the summum bonum, the highest good, which is inevitably pursued in the way most people have always sought God. Only "that which nothing greater can be thought," which is the most minimal definition of the name God, could possibly qualify as the summum bonum, the highest good whom one either pursues or flees, but to whose claims on us no one can be indifferent.[42]

That is why civil society cannot be indifferent to the free pursuit of the One Highest Good. But that free pursuit must admit the right of a free antipursuit if it is to be liberal in the original sense of the term. Therefore, the pursuit of life in its fullness becomes the pursuit of the liberty to pursue happiness as a transcendent reality, who religious people believe is both the origin and the end of human life. "I am the first and I am the last and besides Me there is no god" (Isa. 44:6). The duty of society, both formally and informally, is to enable us to pursue (or flee from) the One who beckons us as the Highest Good. Negatively, that means society does not interfere in that pursuit, either by dictating it specifically or even generally, or by claiming divine prerogatives for itself in the person of either its leaders or its institutions, thus substituting itself for God. Positively, that means that the state sees the pursuit of God being conducted by the majority of its citizens to be in the interest of the common good. Here the common good is itself, somewhat ironically, negative. I think it means that it is in the interest of the state that its citizens look elsewhere for their ultimate happiness, thus having more realistically modest expectations on what the state can do, which is to facilitate its citizens' pursuit of immanent rather than transcendent ends.

By ordinary criteria, which are the only criteria philosophy can employ, we can only postulate that God commands. But by these ordinary criteria, which let us speak of only a trace of the divine in our basic moral norms, we cannot constitute what a real, direct relationship with this God is.[43] As a Jew, I believe that such a relationship, at least for me and my people, obtains in our covenant with God (*brit*) and the law (*torah*) that gives that covenantal relationship its content. Hence my philosophical invocation of God here is my minimal not my maximal existential position. It is like natural law, which is my minimal not my maximal moral position. The name God I have invoked here is not the same name of God I invoke in prayer; and it is not the name of God I would invoke were I required to die as a martyr for the divine Name (*qiddush ha-shem*). It is the same God, but the relationship with this same God is quite different when viewed theologically than when viewed philosophically. As such, God is named differently there than here. Accordingly, though I do not obey God or pray to God in the way a philosopher could postulate God's existence for the sake of a more coherent moral theory, as a philosopher (but not as a theologian), I can speak of this God as the One who entitles or enables or empowers or who makes the assertion of human rights possible in the world. That is why and how I can speak of God in this way without either forcing my faith on anyone or assuming that others hold a faith similar to mine. And as a philosopher, I can do that without compromising my faith by subordinating its direct and ultimate object, who is God, to any worldly power or authority.

But I end with a question: Is religious liberty an issue in a context that is explicitly and not just implicitly religious? Is religious liberty an issue where God is both quoted and addressed continuously? My tentative answer is yes. And that is the subject of chapter 3.

3

Religious Liberty as a Theological Claim

Liberty and Authoritarianism

There is a certain paradox when members of religious communities claim "liberty" in a secular society. The paradox becomes even more acute when the claim for religious liberty is philosophically grounded as a right with which one is endowed by God. The paradox is that the more traditional a religious community is, which means the more it sees itself being under divine authority, the less liberty its members seem to have within the confines of that community itself. Many people would agree with Spinoza—a man who himself left the confines of a traditional religious community—that religion requires *obedience* whereas philosophy requires freedom of thought (*philosophandi libertatem*).[1] Even if a political claim to religious liberty (the subject of chapter 1) is grounded in a philosophical claim to religious liberty (the subject of chapter 2), how can one possibly look for a genuine claim to religious liberty in theology, of all places? How can one look for true liberty in a place where little if any liberty seems to be found? And if claims are rights, didn't rights become a central philosophical and political issue at the time in western history (the eighteenth century) when Europeans (and

Americans) were proclaiming freedom of religion largely to be freedom *from* religion? Didn't the philosophies of the Enlightenment proclaim rights in place of the duties demanded by the ancien régime, one of whose four estates was the Catholic Church? And wasn't the displacement of the Church by the French Revolution even more radical than its displacement of the crown?[2] Moreover, lest one think that an antinomy between liberty and authority is a uniquely Christian problem—or a political problem with Christianity—in a famously influential 1987 article, "Obligation: A Jewish Jurisprudence of the Social Order," the late Yale law professor Robert Cover argued that Judaism, with its emphasis on duty, provides a needed antidote to the overemphasis of rights in liberal democracies.[3] Although, as we have seen in the previous chapter, rights and liberties are not interchangeable terms, nonetheless they are very closely connected.

Yet despite the obvious paradox of what seems to be authority-based (as distinct from reason-based) communities making political and even philosophical claims on secular society, members of these communities do make such claims. And if the 2004 presidential election be any indication of political success, then the great support that George W. Bush received from traditional Protestants, Catholics, and Jews—support that many have seen to be the key factor in his electoral victory—must be interpreted as being the way members of these traditional communities have now chosen to exercise their right to religious liberty. The political exercise of that right is the claim religious people make on society as a whole to adhere to certain moral norms they regard to be universally binding on all people. Nevertheless, the question remains whether these claims to religious liberty are nothing but political ploys, which are only being employed because rights talk is the only talk with which one can make a cogent claim in a secular society, even a claim to *religious* liberty. And that question still remains even when members of religious communities make philosophical arguments to justify their political claims. To many, though, these philosophical arguments seem to be nothing but rationalizations. In other words, these religious claims for liberty could be seen as a device for drawing attention away from the essentially illiberal or antiliberal life that is lived within the religious community itself. Can one ask from others what one is unprepared to give to one's own?

When secularists point out this paradox, they are well advised to present this paradox as an example of hypocrisy. *Hypocrisy* is a term with a religious history; therefore, using it against public religion should get the attention of religious people quicker than the use of some more secular term.[4] Accordingly, aren't religious people being hypocritical when they proclaim liberty for religion in the outside world, but simultaneously exercise more and more authority at home in such activities as heresy hunts and calls for excommunication? Isn't it quite incoherent to make two sets of claims—one at home and another abroad—that basically contradict each other? How can liberty be advocated in one place, yet repressed in another by the very same people?

In the face of this powerful challenge to their credibility, religious people themselves must discover a theological validation of religious liberty from within their own religious traditions, if for no other reason than to indicate that their pursuit of religious liberty is not merely like the statements of certain politicians who speak one way to the world at large and in an altogether opposite way to the folks back home. Surely religious people should not regard their political presence in the world to be some sort of conspiracy anymore than they should regard their employment of philosophy to be mere apologetics. But that requires we once again distinguish theology from philosophy, let alone distinguish theology from political rhetoric. Religious people must look to their respective theologies for their deepest reasons since, for them, theology alone has the most direct access to the word of God, which gives them their fundamental identity in the world and beyond.

Theology and Philosophy

Theology theorizes about the sacred history of a singular community transmitted by and through its faithful members. By "singular community" I mean a community who does not regard itself to be part of a larger social whole, and who regards its singularity as a result of its unique relationship with God. That relationship with God and the relationship among the members of such a community is historical. It is marked by temporal events of the divine-human encounter. It has a story, one that is ongoing. Such a community, then, is grounded in revelation and extends itself historically by its tradition as the transmission and development of what God has revealed to that community in the events of revelation. Theological reflection on religious liberty, as one important moral issue facing that community, should locate religious liberty within the shared history of that community itself. But such reflection can only be done authentically by a thinker who is a willing part of that community. A theologian, then, must be personally committed to the object of his or her theological concern in a way that a philosopher need not be concerned with the object of his or her philosophical concern, at least at the prima facie level. Furthermore, whereas philosophy can intend universal human nature (such as it is at present), theology cannot intend any such universality (at least not at present). Theology, then, can only theorize about the sacred history of one community among others in the world. A theology of *a* history can only aspire to be *the* theology of universal history per se (*l'histoire même* as the French would say) when there will be true universal history at the end time, when God will judge and redeem the entire world and end the world's estrangement from God forever.[5] Nevertheless, since that end time is at present known to God alone, only God could now theorize about it.[6]

Theology, at present anyway, can only presume its existential superiority over any philosophy by asserting that the concrete singularity of its object of concern has more content to offer human beings in their present lives, and that it has offered that content to them in the past as it will offer that content to them in the foreseeable future. The abstract universality any philosophy could propose is just too culturally "thin" to be existentially satisfying, to borrow a term made famous by the cultural anthropologist Clifford Geertz.[7] And when the concrete singularity of theology's concern finally becomes universal at the end time, at this final point theology and philosophy will become one as all creation will become one in true imitation of the oneness of the Creator God. Until that time, though, the claims of theology and the claims of philosophy will remain different: the one more concrete, the other more abstract. But for some of us, who do not consider the claims of theology and the claims of philosophy to be mutually exclusive, these two different claims ought not— and therefore cannot—be contradictory. When these claims are contradictory, one or both of the claims, the theological and/or the philosophical, has been made badly. Furthermore, whereas a philosophical claim of religious liberty can logically undergird a political claim of religious liberty because both of them can be cogently made in the world to the world, theological claims of religious liberty can only be cogently made within one's own traditional community. It is a mistake to see the logical connection that obtains between philosophy and secular politics to obtain between theology and secular politics, too. Unlike philosophy, theology is only *in* the world, not *of* the world. Theology has greater *différance,* to use a term made popular by some Parisian philosophers.

At most, theological claims of religious liberty can make it possible for a theologian to assert philosophical and political claims of religious liberty when speaking in public without contradicting what must be, for a theologian, his or her primary authority. In fact, it is rather easy to say that a religious tradition does not explicitly prohibit, and thus it implicitly permits, its adherents to pursue religious liberty in a secular society. Surely no such prohibition could even be inferred once we learn that a religious tradition does permit its adherents to participate in a secular, multicultural society in good faith. But can we do no more than simply show an absence of contradiction between theology and philosophy on this question of the pursuit of religious liberty? Can we do more than that? Can we discover a positive model that might well be imitated with philosophical persuasion and political profit by analogy? But can we really find any such positive model when we look at the religious data themselves, especially theologically?

Where Is Religious Liberty to Be Found Theologically?

When it comes to "theologizing" about religious liberty within a religious tradition, we have noted that outsiders, especially secularists who place themselves outside any and all religious traditions, do not see enough or, indeed, any religious liberty there at all. But truth be told, even many of those within a religious tradition like Judaism do not see very much or any religious liberty *there* either—which for those of us within that tradition is *here* not there. So, as a Jewish theologian who is committed to religious liberty as a political and a philosophical claim (the subjects of chapters 1 and 2), I must find for myself and for those with whom I converse religious liberty within my own Judaism (Judaism being my commitment, not my possession or invention), and I must find that religious liberty as both fact and norm. In other words, I must now find religious liberty within the tradition having both past precedent and a future trajectory. If I can't do that, then my theological commitment is at loggerheads with my philosophical concerns and my political interests, since in these two areas I have surely found religious liberty as both fact and norm. But living such a divided life can only result in existential incoherence, if not perhaps madness, something any intelligent person should avoid at all costs.

Let us now, at long last, get to the communal history of which theology, in my case Jewish theology, speaks with integrity. Yet we had to first analyze the relation of theology to philosophy and politics lest theology be seen as an escape from ordinary human thought and action rather than a true deepening of them. Even though not *of* the world, theology is *in* the world enough to have to concern itself with such worldly matters as politics and philosophy.

From Slavery to Freedom

The central event of the sacred history of the Jews is Exodus-Sinai, that is the seven-week period beginning with God's taking his people out of Egyptian slavery and culminating with God giving his law (*torah*) to this people assembled at the foot of Mount Sinai. But was there any liberty involved in that eventful experience? Was there any liberty then and there other than God's creative liberty to free this people from slavery or not, and God's creative liberty to reveal his law to this people or not?

Speaking long after the exodus, the prophet Jeremiah says about that event in the name of God: "I grabbed them by the hand in order to bring them out of Egypt" (Jer. 31:31).[8] In other words, as we would say today, God brought Israel out of Egypt "kicking and screaming." As such, we could infer from this that had the people the real liberty to choose whether to stay in Egypt or leave, they would have most likely stayed there. Life in Egypt may have been hard, but it was also comfortable and secure. This explains why the people immediately rebelled against God's covenant and his law. (When Jeremiah says in the next phrase, "they violated My covenant so that I had to overpower them," he probably had in mind the sin of the golden calf, which came on the heels of the Sinaitic revelation.) So, if liberation means going from the power of one master to that of another, then what real difference does this liberation make for those being liberated? Isn't this liberation "empty" like "empty rights," since they are rights the exercise of which is not an expression of any real power on the part of those exercising them?

God had to force the people into the covenant, not trusting them with any real freedom of choice. Thus it seems God had to overcome the resistance of the people, coercively with his greater power, almost as much as God had to overcome the resistance of the pharaoh. Perhaps the people felt that they were mere pawns in a power struggle between the king of Israel and the king of Egypt. Perhaps the people felt that neither God nor the pharaoh truly had what is good for the people at heart. Power can be forced on one by making one accept its decrees, but can one accept decrees to be good for one without being persuaded? Can acceptance of what is good be coerced? By *power* I mean political power, which can only be exercised by persons over other persons, whether the persons exercising that power are human or even divine.

When it comes to the people's reception of God's law at Mount Sinai, the situation does not seem to be any more "liberal." So even though scripture reports that the people at Sinai said: "All that the Lord has spoken we shall do and we shall hear more" (Exod. 24:7), how much of a real choice did they have? Was there any probability of their doing otherwise under those circumstances? Where could they have fled with the wilderness at their backs and burning Mount Sinai in their face? A prominent view in the Talmud is that the people had no real choice, and the ensuing discussion of this view in the Talmud immediately recognizes the theological problem posed thereby.

This view presents itself through an ingenious reading of the scriptural narrative of sinaitic revelation, presuming that the people were not just "standing upright at the foot of the mountain" (Exod. 19:17), but that they were standing "under the mountain." However, how does one possibly stand *under* a mountain? Well, the people are imagined to be standing under Mount Sinai because God held it over their heads, telling them that if they do not accept his Torah right now, "there will be your grave!"[9] Such an immediate choice between life and death gives one no time to deliberate about options and no time to come to a rational deci-

sion. Such a choice seems to lack the true deliberation that Aristotle, for example, thought is necessary for a morally respectable
decision.[10] "To be or not to be," which is the choice God placed
before the people, sounds great in the mouth of Hamlet.[11] But
Shakespeare may well have put such a quote in the mouth of the
procrastinating adolescent prince of Denmark to be ironic; after
all, in the end, Hamlet cannot come to any practical decision at
all. The ultimate gravity of the decision seems to have caused
moral paralysis in poor Hamlet. Faced with such an immediate life-or-death decision, who would have the leisure for moral
deliberation so that he or she could come to a truly rational decision? Yet even without help from Aristotle and Shakespeare,
the Talmud itself records its own moral complaint about this
seeming denial of true human liberty. And it is a moral complaint made against God himself, that is, God as lawgiver. Thus
another rabbi complains that this theologically imaginative proposal of what actually occurred at the time of God's giving and
Israel's receiving of the Torah, is morally problematic, irrespec-
tive of whether it is factually accurate or not. He calls it a "great
indictment of the Torah!"[12]

In concluding the discussion of this story and the great moral
dilemma it raises, a third rabbi suggests that during the people's
exile from their own land after the destruction of the First Temple in 586 B.C., the Jewish people (now a mere two-tribe remnant
of the original twelve tribes of Israel) freely confirmed in exile
what they had originally accepted under duress in the wilderness.[13] But why could the people have freely accepted in Babylonian exile what had to be forced upon them at Mount Sinai? The
answer might be that unlike their situation in the wilderness,
when their only choice was between life and death, in the exile
they had a choice between two ways of life. The city of Babylon offered them options not available in the wilderness, where
just staying alive took all their time and energy. In Babylonia
the people could easily assimilate into the comfortable political, economic, and cultural milieu there—something the other

tribes, the "Ten Lost Tribes of Israel," seemed to have successfully accomplished—or they could follow Ezra and Nehemiah back to the land of Israel. Perhaps the miracle of Jewish survival in exile might well be the reason why the people decided that their survival was due to their ability to live freely according to the Torah. Like all ability, this was seen to be a good gift from God, a gift to which the people could truly respond with the greatest of all freedoms: the freedom to love God responsively and responsibly. A phenomenology of the experience of being commanded shows that being commanded presupposes genuine freedom of choice as its precondition, a point made by the greatest medieval Jewish jurist-theologian, Moses Maimonides.[14]

The Jewish people not only returned *voluntarily* to their ancestral homeland but, much more importantly, they returned to the Torah and made it their national constitution in an unprecedented way. Even when the people enjoyed national sovereignty during the days of the First Temple, the written Torah does not seem to have functioned as the ultimate national authority—an ultimate authority the Torah seems to have gained only with the voluntary return of the Jewish people under the leadership of Ezra the Scribe. Moreover, this free reacceptance of the Torah outside the borders of the land of Israel meant that even the Jews who chose not to return to the land of Israel by remaining in the Babylonian Diaspora (or anywhere else in the world) are still considered to be part of the national covenant (*brit*) and its law (*torah*). Thus the theological difference between Israeli Jews and Diaspora Jews is, to this very day, one of degree rather than one of kind. Israeli Jews can observe more of the commandments of the Torah, since some of the Torah's commandments may only be practiced within the land of Israel.[15] Nevertheless, short of the coming of the Messiah, even Israeli Jews cannot keep *all* of the commandments (like those pertaining to the Temple), and even non-Israeli, Diaspora Jews cannot regard themselves to be bound by *none* of the commandments. All Jews are equally members of the same covenant in principle; and in fact, all Jews who voluntarily take upon themselves the "yoke of the commandments" (*ol shel mitsvot*) function equally as active members of the same covenant, wherever they happen to live. Living in the land of Israel is always preferable, but Israeli Jews do not have a monopoly on the covenant. Their position is optimal, not exclusive.

One could well ask: Why did the people first have the law forced upon them rather than having it persuasively offered to them later to freely accept or reject, as was the case subsequently? The answer might be that the people could not very well choose a law of whose rule they had no previous experience. In other words, isn't our most basic moral choice the choice to reconfirm or deny a law that we could not have freely accepted or rejected in childhood? (And even when we reject the morality of our childhood, do we not inevitably accept another morality from someone else's childhood?) Aristotle was no doubt correct when he insisted that ethical theory, which includes the criteria of moral deliberation and choice, cannot be taught to those too young to have had sufficient moral experience.[16] And indeed, even when proposing his idea of moral autonomy as the essential form of morality, Kant still maintained that he was only rationally reconfirming the content of morality as traditionally received.[17] Even Kant did not presume to say that human beings create the actual content of their own morality *de novo*. (Kant was not Nietzsche.)[18] How much more so is this true, then, for those of us who do not propose autonomy as even the formal basis of morality.

By deciding to reconstitute themselves to be a covenanted nation governed according to divine law revealed in the Torah, the Jewish people exercised religious liberty collectively. Even though God and Israel are not equal partners in the covenant, as would be the case were the covenant a contract, nonetheless the Jewish people's voluntary reacceptance (or reconfirmation) of the covenant and its law enables the covenant to be politically effective in a way it had not been effective in the days of the First Temple. During that earlier period, the chief efforts of the prophets had been to wean the people away from following the idolatrous ways of their pagan neighbors. There seemed to be little energy or opportunity left to govern the people according to the more specific precepts of the Torah then.[19] But now, with the radically different cultural and political situation of the people after their voluntary return to the land of Israel from Babylon, the scribal and rabbinic successors of the earlier prophets were able to allow the voluntary reacceptance of the Torah by the people to make a practical difference. In fact, there is an opinion in the Talmud that idolatry ceased to be a social problem during the days of the Second Temple; hence the more mundane moral problems that concern law could now receive fuller attention.[20]

Religious Liberty as a Collective Right

Now let us turn to how the voluntary reacceptance or reconfirmation of the Torah by the Jewish people functioned as an exercise of religious liberty at both the collective and the individual levels.

My example of religious liberty as a collective right comes from the period of the formation of the Talmud, roughly between the first and fifth centuries. Nevertheless, although the origins of this right are ancient, its exercise has not ceased up until the present day and, it is hoped, into the foreseeable future.

Religious liberty was exercised then by innovative reinterpretation *of* scriptural law and by innovative supplementation *to* that law. In both cases, a learned elite as well as the populace had to be persuaded to freely accept what had been newly reinterpreted and legislated.[21] As for God's explicit approval, in the absence of prophecy, the community will have to wait for that divine approval from the Messiah or Elijah, the messianic "advance man."[22] Nevertheless, the exercise of that exegetical and legislative liberty does not have to wait for the coming of the Messiah; that liberty functions today in traditional Jewish communities who voluntarily regard themselves as subject to the governance of the law: the *Halakhah*. Thus, although its beginnings are ancient and its ultimate validation is eschatological, the free reenunciation of the law and the free submission to the law is normative (and not just past fact or future hope), and *normative Judaism* is alive and well in the (growing) traditional Jewish community. By *traditional community*, I mean those Jews who accept scriptural revelation as truth and who accept the authority of Jewish law as it has developed up until the present day.

Whether engaged in reinterpretation or supplementary legislation, in an atmosphere of considerable discursive freedom rabbis attempt to persuade each other of what the correct interpretation and supplementation of the law should be. There is, moreover, considerable freedom in the range of hermeneutical methods and the types of arguments that may be employed in this discursive context, a context like what the philosopher Jürgen Habermas calls an "ideal community of communication."[23] Furthermore, from the talmudic texts we see that this whole process of normative innovation is not just the exercise of liberty by and within a learned elite, a rabbinical oligarchy, even though this elite has been remarkably free of exclusions due to class or ancestry. Rather, in order to be intellectually cogent, let alone politically effective, this whole exegetical and legislative process has had to take popular usage into immediate and continual consideration. Thus, any seemingly radical reinterpretation of "law on the books" must be a formalization of what the people have already been freely practicing informally.[24]

Even when a rabbinical figure of the brilliance of the second century sage Akibah ben Joseph proposes something new with dazzling hermeneutical power, his colleagues nonetheless warn him that they cannot accept the practical conclusion of his reasoning unless it already confirms long accepted popular practice.[25] As the Talmud puts it more than once: "Go see how the people are conducting themselves"—that is, go see the ordinary conduct of the people who have bound themselves to a consistent observance of the law in general before the law can be effectively decided.[26] But it also seems that if for whatever reason the learned proposal, even with rabbinical consensus, does not have popular acceptance already, its rabbinical proponents must be able to persuade enough people to adopt that proposal subsequently. Indeed, that is why the rulings of Akibah's predecessors of the School of Hillel became the norm: they either had much popular precedent from the past on their side or they won people over to their side by their present exercise of political persuasion.[27]

To be sure, this popular consensus was not determined by anything like a formal plebiscite such as we have today in popular elections. Rather, it was determined by a sense of overall popular acceptance, which minimally might be nothing more than the absence of any real opposition to a particular ruling. But more often than not, an innovative ruling did require explicit agreement of a majority, and that majority had to be more than 51 percent. In the absence of such free popular consent, the law remains at the level of *stare decisis*. The status quo, then, can only be overcome by something akin to what Catholics have called *consensus fidelium:* the agreement of most of the faithful.[28] In the absence of the means of physical or political coercion, that consensus would seem to require reasoned persuasion to be morally effective. It must be presented and accepted as a desideratum.

Legal exegesis does have its limits, however. There are too many situations where to get a ruling, the law would have to be stretched in ways too far-fetched to be credulous, resulting in the bad reputation of being called "hair-splitting."[29] Furthermore, the popular consensus needed to make such legal exegesis practically effective in the community seems to be a consensus from the past, a past that not only has a vote but seems to have a veto as well. As such, the customary past seems to hinder the religious liberty of the present community here and now. Indeed, there are limitations on the interpretative process, called *midrash*, we have been looking at, especially the veto power of past rulings that limits the religious liberty of the present community.[30]

Later in the talmudic period the rabbis distinguished between law derived by the exegesis of codified law and law proposed by legislation (*taqqanah*). These are the "rabbinic commandments" (*mitsvot de-rabbanan*). Exegesis derives new rules *from* old written law; legislation proposes changing the law either by addition or subtraction. Here the rabbis had to persuade the people that these changes were for their benefit, and they had to show that these changes did not uproot the law entirely.[31]

Law proposed by legislation has two advantages over law exegetically derived. First, it involves greater intellectual freedom: the freedom to speculate, which can explore more options than textual interpretation alone. That is because legislative proposal, when intelligently conducted, requires a bold discovery of what the ends of the law are, and these ends are frequently implicit rather than explicit in the text of scripture itself. Although a theological enterprise, one can see much philosophical affinity in the speculation about ends. It is teleology. Indeed, the most astute of rabbinic minds would probably agree with Aristotle that teleology constitutes thinking at its highest point. (Indeed, Maimonides made much good use of Aristotelian teleology, especially in his ethical and legal thought, that is, in his practical theology.)[32] Secondly, rabbinic legislation, much more than rabbinic legal exegesis, must recognize the liberty of the present community to accept or reject what it proposes to be praxis.[33]

This greater requirement to recognize popular liberty can be seen in a pivotal principle of rabbinic legislation: "No rule is to be made unless the majority of the members of the community are prepared to live by it."[34] Here again, we need to remember that this is determined by an informal but overwhelming popular consensus, not the arithmetic one vote more than 50 percent that formally determines who or what wins in a popular election. But how do we know that this majority actually obtains? We know it when we see that the proposal has indeed been put into practice among a vast number of the people.[35] The question, though, is whether the free will of this popular majority determines what the law is to be in and for a later generation. As far as the rabbis who made the law are concerned, at least in principle, a later rabbinic body can overturn the legislative decision of an earlier rabbinic body.[36] Nevertheless, in the absence of a Jewish supreme court, that procedure *de jure* is almost impossible to explicitly utilize de facto. Instead, radical judicial reinterpretation is what has usually had to suffice for repeal. Often it is quite tortured in its logic, especially in its use of what can only be seen as highly tenuous analogies, analogies that try to turn past cases into ready precedents for current situations calling for legal judgment.

However, what about the consent of the people? Is the freedom of the people in the present effectively curtailed, in fact vetoed, by a past majority's free decision? Some have answered yes to this question. But Maimonides seems to have answered no. He suggested that if a practice decided upon by a previous majority has now fallen into disuse by the present majority of the people, then this practical omission—this "sitting by and doing nothing" as the Talmud puts it elsewhere—is de facto repeal of the earlier rabbi-made law.[37] Here, formal repeal by a rabbinical body does not seem necessary to alleviate the present generation of any sin of omission. (Such would not be the case, however, where there has been practical omission of a scriptural law. In this case, the rabbis are required to admonish the people to return to the law they have heretofore neglected.) Accordingly, here the rabbis may "leave the people alone" as the Talmud puts it, namely, to leave the people be in what they have chosen not to practice.[38] In other words, the people may choose to disassociate themselves from an earlier (man-made) ruling, something they surely may not do with natural law or with divinely revealed law.

I would like to suggest that this is a prime example of the theological sanction of the collective exercise of religious liberty. Nevertheless, since the dawn of modernity, we usually designate religious liberty to be an individual's right. So we need to find an example of where the tradition has recognized such an individual right, whether de jure or only de facto.

Religious Liberty as an Individual Right

My example of religious liberty as an individual right comes from the Middle Ages. But like the collective right discussed above, the exercise of this right extends far beyond the period in which it came to the fore in Jewish thinking and practice. Like the previously noted collective right, this individual right is still an option for Jews today.

The greatest problem facing medieval Jewish communities was the ever-present threat of apostasy. Being a small, vulnerable minority, whether in Christian societies or in Muslim societies, there was always the danger to the community that some of its members would choose to renounce the community and formally identify with the majority religion and culture. This was an especially acute danger since both Christians and Muslims, *mutatis mutandis*, were actively proselytizing Jews. To be sure, there were times when Jews were forced to convert to Christianity or to Islam, that is, when fanatical Christian or Muslim groups, unable to tolerate any religious or cultural difference in their midst, gave Jews the choice of conversion or death. This happened in European Christendom during the First Crusade in the eleventh century. At this time, entire Jewish communities in the Rhineland chose death, sometimes even by their own hand, rather than abandon Judaism by converting to Christianity. Theirs was the choice of martyrdom, what Jewish tradition calls "sacrificing one's life for the sanctity of the divine Name." And although a Jew is supposed to choose death over forced conversion, the tradition was extremely reticent to condemn those not having the courage to properly make that awful choice. That reticence translated into extreme leniency in welcoming back to the community those Jewish "converts" who were eventually able to escape their religious captors and come back home.[39]

In ordinary matters of law, Jewish tradition regards acts committed under duress not to be culpable after the fact.[40] Such acts are considered to be accidents beyond normal human control. The duty of martyrdom is an exception to this rule, since the would-be martyr does have a choice before the fact, however awful that choice is. As such, the would-be martyr is unlike the victim of an accident, whose unfortunate circumstances led to his or her becoming an inadvertent instrument of harm to another person or another person's property. (The choice of apostasy, on the other hand, involves mortal harm to one's own soul.)[41] Nevertheless, medieval apostasy, more often than not, was a choice made under less gruesome circumstances. There were Jews who were able to make a free decision to convert to either Christianity or Islam, and they were able to do so with the requisite deliberation that is available to one when, so to speak, a knife is not at one's throat. Such persons were able to weigh their options and make a choice that was not one of physical life or death. Accordingly, their culpability was greater than those terrified into apostasy.

Whether these willing apostates chose to abandon Judaism because they actually believed the theological claims of the other religion trump those of Judaism, especially for the sake of the world to come, or whether they chose to abandon the Jewish people because the political status of being a Christian or a Muslim was more attractive in this world, that motivation surely varies from case to case. And in the end, the true motivation for that choice is known only to the person who made that choice, and to God who judges that choice as God judges all our choices. "Humans only see appearances, but God sees the heart" (1 Sam. 16:7).[42]

This, however, only tells us about the problem of the individual Jewish apostate and the problem Jews believe God has with the apostate. It does not tell us about the problem the Jewish community has with this kind of person. The community is the third component of the covenant between God and Israel. (One can see the covenant as being the interaction between God, individual Jews, and the Jewish community.) So how is the Jewish community itself to deal with the choice of one of its members to leave Judaism and the Jewish people for another theologico-political identity in the world? And this question touches upon the prior theological question: How much liberty is involved in one's becoming a Jew? Hence we have the opposite theological question: Is there any liberty, any right, any entitlement to cease being a Jew by becoming someone else?

When looking at the event of Exodus-Sinai, the founding event of the covenant between God and Israel (what much later came to be known as "Judaism"), we have seen how the original status of the Jews as God's covenanted people was forced upon them. The people themselves originally became "Israel" involuntarily. For individual Jews, this means that their being born of a Jewish mother determines their Jewish status until the moment of their death.[43] And what could be more involuntary than one's birth and who one's parents are?[44] (According to Jewish tradition, though, certain Jews who have freely and publicly rejected basic Jewish dogmas like that of the revelation of the Torah as God's law, will be excluded from eschatological Israel: they will lose their "portion" in the world to come, which is to be populated by "all—that is, *most of*—Israel," along with the "righteous of the nations of the world," who are those gentiles who have positively responded to God's law as it has been revealed to them in this world.) [45]

To be sure, Jews are not being hypocritical by protesting when Jews are forced to convert to some other religion, since Jewish law judges a forced conversion to Judaism to be invalid.[46] (Even non-Jewish infants adopted by Jews and converted to Judaism in childhood have the right to renounce what was done on their

behalf when they reach adulthood.)[47] Nevertheless, even though
the decision of a gentile to convert to Judaism has to be voluntary, a Jewish court is under no obligation to automatically accept such a willing candidate for conversion. In other words, the
free choice of a gentile to convert to Judaism is a necessary but
not sufficient condition of his or her becoming a Jew. In rabbinic
literature, one does not "convert" (*mitgayyer*) by oneself to Judaism; instead, one "is converted" *(nitgayyer)* to Judaism by the
community.[48] It is like one "being born," as distinct from "giving
birth" to oneself. In essence, then, a convert to Judaism is almost
as much *elected* into the covenant as is someone who is born a
Jew.[49] Yet the requirement of free choice on the part of any gentile to present himself or herself as a *candidate for conversion* is
a good example of the right to religious liberty being recognized
by the Jewish tradition, at least as far as it is the right of any gentile to choose whatever religion he or she wants to follow.

The real question, though, is whether there is any official
Jewish recognition of the right of a Jew to leave Judaism and the
Jewish people for some other identity in the world. Can a Jew
leave Judaism for a gentile community like a gentile can leave
his or her gentile community for Judaism? If the answer to this
question is no, then we have the great irony of Judaism recognizing that gentiles have greater rights to religious liberty than
Jews have.

Already in the Talmud it is recognized that once a gentile has
been converted to Judaism, the fact of that conversion is irrevocable.[50] The conversion is irrevocable even were the new convert to revert to his gentile religion immediately following the
completion of the requisite rites of conversion. But what about
those born Jewish? One could say that since conversion presupposes there are already born Jews to accept the convert into *their*
community, then if a convert may not become a gentile again,
surely a born Jew may not become a gentile ever, since he or she
is more originally Jewish than any convert.[51] But on the other
hand, one could say that since a convert should be required to

live up to the unconditional commitment made by the act of being converted to Judaism willingly, why should a born Jew not
have the same right as a gentile to renounce an identity forced
upon him by the involuntary event of birth? Although neither
argument is actually proposed in the classical Jewish sources
as far as I know, these arguments could have well been made
in the great debate about whether or not one can convert out
of Judaism. This debate was very much in the air for a period
of time stretching from the fifth to the eleventh century. Some
authorities ruled that one could leave Judaism just as one could
be expelled from the Jewish people. Other authorities rule that
once a Jew always a Jew.[52]

For almost all Jews, this question was resolved in the eleventh
century by the great French-Jewish exegete and jurist Rashi. In
a responsum on the subject of Jewish apostasy, Rashi invoked a
talmudic dictum: "Even when a Jew has sinned, he is still a Jew
[*yisrael hu*]."[53] Even though the original meaning of this dictum
might have been a polemic against Christian supersessionism,
which asserts that God has permanently rejected the Jewish
people from the collective status of being *elected Israel,* Rashi interprets the word *Israel* to apply to individual Jews.[54] Even for the
worst sin possible, the sin of apostasy, the apostate is still considered to be a Jew—at least while he or she is still alive in this
world. Apostasy is akin to idolatry in that both are designated as
forbidden "strange worship" (*avodah zarah*).[55] This would seem
to deny any recognition of a Jew being able—that is, having the
liberty—to leave Judaism and the Jewish people with theological impunity. (The current question of those Jews who become
Christians, but who still want to be part of the Jewish people,
poses a different problem than the one faced by Rashi and his
contemporaries.) That lack of what we might call "exit-liberty"
is, of course, the conclusion one must draw when looking at
Rashi's authoritative ruling *de jure*. (Here again, this ruling became practically operative because of its popular acceptance.)
However, how did this ruling play out in fact?

I submit that in fact, if not in principle, Jewish authorities did recognize the right of a Jew to leave Judaism and the Jewish people. How? They simply let apostates leave and did little or nothing to force them to come back to Judaism and the Jewish people. To be sure, any active Jewish campaign to bring apostates back home would have been quite dangerous in medieval Christian and Muslim societies where Jews were often prohibited from accepting converts from Christianity or Islam, much less proselytizing Christians or Muslims (even though there is historical evidence that both activities were done by Jews covertly). Jews could be converted by others, but could not convert others in turn, even if these "others" had formerly lived a Jewish life. (Double standards like this help explain why Jews were so enthusiastic about the end of "Christendom" in Europe beginning in the eighteenth century.) Nevertheless, even when Jews had the opportunity to bring apostates back, they usually chose not to do so. Thus, for example, the Jewish community had a solemn obligation to redeem Jews sold into slavery so that these unfortunates would not be lost to the Jewish people. But that obligation does not extend to Jewish apostates.[56] Here it seems that the community felt no responsibility for Jews who did not want to remain Jews. If some Jews want to be gentiles, then let their new community assume responsibility for their welfare.

Jews have also felt an obligation, though, to rescue Jewish children raised as gentiles when these children were too young to have had the power of consent.[57] This became an urgent task after the Holocaust in cases of Jewish children raised as gentiles by gentiles who thereby rescued them from certain death at the hands of the Nazis. In this context, I might add, Jews have good reason to thank those Christians, especially those Christian clergy who helped some of those Jewish children who were placed by their parents with Christian families (and who in some cases were baptized without the consent of their Jewish parents) return to their parents after World War II. What a significant, and no doubt theologically motivated, recognition of the right of religious liberty of parents from another community!

There are many examples of where Jewish apostates were treated *as if* they were gentiles. The most important difference between these apostates and gentiles is that if an apostate wants to return to Judaism and the Jewish people, the community is obligated to reaccept him or her with no rite of conversion or reconversion necessary.[58] The most that is to be done in such cases of Jews returning to Judaism is that a rite of purification, which is to be explicitly differentiated from the rite of conversion, is to be performed. That might well be for psychological reasons rather than for strictly theological ones, namely, to ease the guilt a former apostate intensely feels. (As a rabbi, I have dealt with such cases personally.) To be sure, politically speaking, the apostate did leave the extant Jewish community. But, metaphysically speaking, a Jew can only leave the Jewish people when permanently expelled from the community of Israel in the world to come. In this world, though, an apostate is only AWOL: absent without leave. But in fact, all that means is that Jews do not give any apostate a farewell party.[59] Rather, Jews should remind apostates of their right to return to the Jewish people and Judaism, no questions asked, as it were. Apostates may have gone out the front door and locked it behind themselves, but the back door always remains unlocked for them. Nevertheless, their decision must be respected insofar as any attempt to coerce them back into Judaism is, to my mind, the moral if not the legal equivalent of a forced conversion of a gentile to Judaism.

For reasons more psychological than theological perhaps, it seems the Jewish community did not want to hold prisoner, so to speak, anyone who did not want to be there in good faith. And in a more strictly theological vein: just as the covenant between God and Israel did not become fully effective until the Jewish people voluntarily reaccepted it in the exile and during the days of the Second Temple, so is the covenant between God and individual Jews not fully effective unless an individual Jew wants to be in the covenant under no external duress. That is why Jews have welcomed willing gentile converts *to* Judaism but have not detained those Jews wanting to depart *from* Judaism. Furthermore, whereas willing converts are a good influence on those who are born Jews by reminding them that Judaism is too good to ever be taken for granted, unwilling Jews, whose rebellion extends to the far point of apostasy, are a bad influence by showing them that Judaism is an unwanted burden, if not a curse. But the de facto recognition of the right to radically leave Judaism does not entail any communal duty or even communal permission to approve of those who have chosen to exercise that right. Error does have rights in the political sense, but error cannot be committed with ultimate impunity. The judgment of apostates and their claims is ultimately the business of God alone because, in essence, apostasy is really not about this world, which is the only world about which and in which humans can judge other humans.

The Metaphysical Question of Freedom

If there is religious liberty within a religious tradition like Judaism, then why have so many modern Jews departed from any real connection to God's covenant with Israel and its Torah? Do not most of them claim that their rejection of the Torah is due to their quest for the greater liberty of the world? That explains why modern Jews rarely leave Judaism for another religion. In fact, they often insist that Christianity (or Islam) is just as "authoritarian" as is their ancestral Judaism. Of course, traditional Jews like myself attribute this departure for secularism to a desire for religious and moral license, and we believe that our secularist brothers and sisters do not understand that true liberty is never an end in itself, but it is always for the sake of what transcends its own exercise.[60] But perhaps there is another answer to the charge that Judaism limits one's freedom. The answer is metaphysical; it is from the most theoretical aspect of theology, somewhat different from the practical or political side of theology I have been making use of in this chapter. Being metaphysical, I don't suspect it will make much of a political difference in the world. That notwithstanding, it might have some theological cogency for those who seek such cogency.

Liberty or freedom is usually measured by the number of options available to it: more options more freedom; fewer options less freedom. But on that score, license wins because its range of options is greatest. That is why in this libertarian (often hedonistic) view of life, any restraint of one's range of options might be a political necessity, but it is not an existential desideratum. However, liberty or freedom can also be measured by the depth of the options offered: the deeper the options the greater the freedom to choose one or the other; the more shallow the options the more shallow the freedom to choose one or the other. Thus philosophy offers more freedom of choice than does politics because, as we have seen, philosophy offers us the choice of justice or injustice, whereas politics only offers us the choice of good or bad tactics. So, on that score, theology offers us the most freedom of choice possible in this world because it offers us the deepest choice possible. What is that choice? It is the choice between the worship of God and the worship of what is not-God. Who is not-God? It is ourselves when we set ourselves up to be God's equal. The serpent's offer to the first man and the first woman is the offer of original sin: "You shall be like God!" (Gen. 3:5). But if humans are God's equal, then God is no longer God; God is no longer "the first and the last besides Me there is no god" (Isa. 44:6). God can surely tolerate an other not opposed to his kingship. After all, didn't God create a world apart from himself so as to rule over it? "Everyone called by My name, for My glory I have created them" (Isa. 43:7). But could God tolerate an equal whose very assertion of his or her equality would destroy God's kingship? (Thus Nietzsche was right about atheism being deicide.)[61] Unlike the choice between tactics that politics gives us, and unlike the choice between principles that philosophy gives us, this theological choice is the deepest and the most direct choice possible for humans. We make it every time we are confronted by God's direct commandments. With full consciousness of what this choice involves, we are brought right before God. No greater liberty could possibly be known. Furthermore, the alternatives in philosophy and in politics are something positive and its privation: justice or injustice; good tactics or bad tactics. The theological alternative, though, is between God and his negating rival, a rival who is not himself or herself a mere negation. That rival, then, is not Nothing or "nothingness." That radical evil is most definitely someone. So, the theological choice is between two real, opposing alternatives: two alternatives where one alternative is not simply inferred as the lack of the other as in the Platonic formula: "evil is the privation of good."[62]

When we exercise this metaphysical liberty, we are in a better position to appreciate that the philosophical choice of justice or injustice is most reasonably made by those who know what is greater than worldly justice and, therefore, do not make unreasonable demands for it nor do they despair of making those demands at all. And we are in a better position to understand for whom we make the political claim to religious liberty, and that all the toil involved in making that claim is a very small price to pay for what we receive and will receive from the ultimate object of that claim of all claims made in this world—God. Surely, the greatness of our claim to religious liberty in this world is best appreciated from a theological perspective.

Part Two

4

Religious Liberty in a Secular Society

The Current Threat to Religious Liberty

Make no mistake about it, religious liberty is being seriously threatened today. To cite just one recent example, take the case of Trinity Western University in British Columbia, where the university had to defend in court the right of their graduates to be hired as public school teachers. That right was challenged by, among others, the teachers union in B.C., because these Trinity Western graduates have been taught, as part of the overall religious vocation of this university, that homosexual behavior is morally wrong. Apparently, what Trinity Western thinks is morally wrong is now "politically incorrect"—at least in some powerful circles. Even the fact that these teacher candidates are not being hired to teach sexual ethics, and that they are committed not to discriminate against any of their students because of sexual behavior, did not prevent their opponents from challenging their fitness to be teachers in secular, public schools. Fortunately—some might say providentially—Trinity Western won its case in court.

Nevertheless, we are all aware how partial and temporary that judicial victory is when viewed within the larger context of the present state of society and culture. So, Trinity Western's judicial victory should not be an occasion of self-congratulation as much as a warning for us to become fully aware of what we are up against. The threat to religious liberty is by no means a uniquely Canadian problem. Indeed, it is a problem facing every religious community in every constitutional democracy in the world. And even more than we need to be aware of *what* we are up against, we need to understand *how* we are to argue for our religious liberty in a secular society. In the end, that means we need to know *why* we claim religious freedom to be the first right in a secular society, one that trumps all other rights.

We need to make this case for both religious and secular reasons. That in itself goes against the assumption, one might even say the "dogma," of our secularist opponents, since in their view a reason can only be *either* religious *or* secular, but never *both* religious *and* secular in tandem. Furthermore, for these secularists, what is religious must be kept totally private and what is secular must be kept public. However, morality is by definition public since it pertains to relations that are *plural,* that is, relations between two or more persons. Therefore, according to secularist logic, no religious reason can be consistently public as well.[1] And, going to the next step in this logical trajectory, that means that no religious reason can ever be invoked in any moral debate, especially moral debates that have political and legal consequences. To deprive any religious tradition its right to make moral claims on its members, let alone make moral claims on other citizens based on an idea of natural law, is antireligious persecution. Indeed, in some sectors of society, a moral argument can be made on the basis of almost any belief system *except* a religious one.

The philosophical task, then, is to show that this privatization of religion is essentially undemocratic, both in terms of the idea of democracy and in terms of the experience of democracy. Privacy is essentially an entitlement from society, something society subsequently gives its members under its own conditions.

Freedom of religion, conversely, is something the members of society already have, and which society is duty bound to enforce on their behalf. When a democratic society sees freedom of religion to be its entitlement—that is, an entitlement like the freedom of privacy—it ceases to be democratic because religion can only be a department of a society that claims existential ultimacy for its own demands on its citizens. But that type of society cannot be—or ceases to be—a democracy inasmuch as a democracy respects the right of its citizens to make that kind of ultimate commitment somewhere higher than any human regime can ever be. A democracy can truly accept its human limitations best when it realizes it is not divine, not even God's chosen messenger. Only a society making divine claims on its citizens can *grant* them freedom of religion instead of *recognizing* the freedom of religion which is theirs, as Scripture puts it, "from another place" (Esther 4:14). But such a society, as the reign of terror after the French Revolution of 1789 and after the Russian Revolution of 1917 and after the German Revolution of 1933 showed, ceases to be a democracy. That is the secular reason for the priority of freedom of religion *in* but never *from* a democracy. Religious freedom is something citizens bring *to* a democracy. It is not only their claim upon democratic society; it is their gift *for* it as well.

Our task, then, is not only to show the incoherence, both logical and historical, of the privatization of religion advocated by our secularist opponents, but even more so to show how our understanding of the relation of various social spheres with one another is more coherent in terms of its use of logic and its use of history. We need to show how one's religion makes a social claim on one that is prior to the social claim made by any secular state; indeed, how one's religion validates one's acceptance of secular authority in a way that secular authority can never validate one's acceptance of membership in the elect people of God. Thus we need to show that the public-private division assumed to be the basis of discussions of religious freedom is not where the question of religious liberty is to be located. Instead, religious liberty is the right of a religious community to govern the morality of its members without any secular coercion. In other words, freedom of religion is my right to be a member or not to be a member of a religious community, and thus freely submit myself to its moral authority. However, freedom of religion becomes what could be called an "empty right" if the religious community I freely choose to join does not have the liberty to morally govern me and my fellow community members. Therefore, my right of religious freedom presupposes the communal right of a religious community to exercise its moral authority. That moral authority is its liberty. For secular purposes, it is enough to look upon this as the right to communal autonomy. For religious purposes, though, we must look to this authority as the communal duty to interpret and apply the law of God which has been revealed to the community and which has been transmitted by its own tradition.

Without that prior communal liberty, my right to religious freedom could only be my right to found my own *individual* religion for myself alone. Yet, most people, whether religious or not, would not regard this extreme individualism, this theological solipsism, to be what any religion could possibly mean. I suspect that this is what "spirituality," which some people today advocate as a substitute for "institutional religion," means. But, would not most religious people indeed see one of the main tasks of religion to be to form the type of community that overcomes such individual isolation both from God and from one's fellow humans, beginning with one's fellow believers? So, one could say that this type of freedom of religion is unintelligible because it is freedom *for* a religion that no one could recognize to be a religion. Even though the philosopher William James famously said that "religion is what one does with his solitude," most of us would regard that to be the most erroneous thing that James or any philosopher could possibly say about any religion.[2] Therefore, the practice of a religion is just as public as any secular activity precisely because it is a communal practice. In fact, religion is *the* most public human practice imaginable. Indeed, religion might be seen as the ultimate invasion of one's privacy. That is why commandments, which make a claim on my action in relation to others, are such an essential part of what most people would consider a religion. A "god" who doesn't make public demands of us doesn't seem to be much of a *God* at all.

A democracy need only ensure that no adult citizen has his or her privacy invaded by any religion without his or her consent. Accordingly, a democracy must protect itself from being seized by any religion in order to be the instrument of its social coercion. Most Christians and Jews in North America—and I think most Muslims and Hindus too—have very good religious reasons for not wanting their religious practices to be coerced by or even through secular authority. All we ask is that our communal religious practices, stemming from our communal faith, be respected by secular authority. Historically, that secular authority itself has been authorized by a citizenry, the majority of whom claim to be religious in one way or another.

The Marc Hall Case

Since it is always good, whenever possible, to focus a moral debate on a particular case, one that is as near at hand as possible, I would like to look at a recent case, one that took place in my own province of Ontario, but one that has received wide attention throughout Canada, and far beyond. The case of Marc Hall and his fight with the Durham Catholic District School Board will help illustrate my philosophical points. Not being a lawyer, I do not presume to discuss the legalities of this case as it was recently argued before the Ontario Superior Court. Instead, I want to discuss this case as it involves basic questions of political philosophy. Indeed, the intelligent formulation of opinion in a democracy, which many see to be the very heart of what it means to be a democratic society, depends on such public philosophi-

cal discussion inasmuch as a democracy requires the continuing rational consent of its citizens as to the way it is governed.
Without such regular consent, and the rational discussion it
presupposes, a democracy quickly becomes the tyranny of some
ruling elite, usually one that is not elected by the people. So,
for my text, I will not take a transcript of the hearing before the
Ontario Superior Court but, rather, a newspaper report that ap-
peared in the *National Post and Opinion* on May 18, 2002, written by Sarah Schmidt.[3]

The case involved the refusal of the Durham Catholic District
School Board to allow Marc Hall, a practicing homosexual, to es-
cort his lover, Jean-Paul Dummond (coyly referred to as his "boy-
friend"), to the annual prom held for graduating seniors by the
Monsignor John Pereyma Catholic School in Oshawa, Ontario.
Apparently, a student at the school may bring a nonstudent to
the prom as his or her date. Hall, age seventeen, was a student
at this Catholic high school; Dummond, age twenty-one, was
not. Hall and his supporters appealed the decision of the school
board to the secular court. The secular court ruled in favor of
Hall and ordered the school board to allow him to attend the
prom and participate in the dance with Dummond as his date.
In many secular circles—and even in some religious ones—Marc
Hall's victory has become a cause of great celebration.

As a Jewish Ontarian, I take special interest in this practical
question inasmuch as the Jewish community of Ontario is now
developing a coalition with the Catholic Church to include the
right to a Jewish education within that constitutional right previously recognized only for Catholic schools by the province in
both accreditation and funding. (Next to the Catholic Church,
the Jewish community educates the largest number of students
in religious day schools. In Toronto, the largest Jewish community in Canada, around 40 percent of all Jewish children are edu-
cated in these religious day schools.)

In her article in the *National Post*, Sarah Schmidt astutely
frames the question as to whether the "constitutional right to

a Catholic education, afforded to Ontarians in 1867 [the year of the Canadian Confederation] . . . trumps the rights of gays and lesbians to live free from discrimination."

We now need to sort out what is meant by the rights of gays and lesbians not to be discriminated against, and what is meant by the right to a religious education—that is, in lieu of a secular or public school education—and how one right can or should trump another right.

Rights or Entitlements

Unlike the right of religious freedom—that is, the right to be included in the religious liberty of one's own traditional community—the right to engage in various sexual practices is not prior to the authority of the state but subsequent to it. In other words, it is an entitlement *from* the state, not an *inalienable* right (to use the language of the Declaration of Independence).[4] As such, the state has the right to regulate, even prohibit, sexual acts under certain circumstances. Proof of this is that the state prohibits sexual activity between adults and children, and it prohibits coercive or dangerous sexual activity between adults. And in fact, the only reason most people think that the state should not interfere in sexual activity between consenting adults is because no public good is served by such public interference in what consenting adults do in private. We do not want a society where the state spends time and energy snooping in most people's beds. That would create more problems than it would solve. The repeal of laws prohibiting the sale and even the use of artificial birth control devices is a prime example of that removal of the authority of the state from people's beds.

Like the right to privacy, which is in truth the entitlement *of* privacy, the exercise of this sexual right is contingent on interests of public good. And indeed, there could be interests of public good that would require the interference of the state even in the private sexual activity of consenting adults. For example, one could argue that the state has the right to prohibit sexual activity between two consenting adults, one of whom is HIV positive, saying that in the interest of public health, sexual practices that result in the likely spread of serious disease in society should be banned—if for no other reason than those who will suffer from the disease will certainly tax the resources of the public health-care system. The prevention of the spread of disease is most definitely a social duty.

Of course, one could say that the state has the right to interfere in religious practices that are unhealthy and pose a threat to public safety. But what would such practices be? Our moral conceptions of the right to life and the right to the protection of life, even to the right to the enhancement of life. have all been accepted by the religions practiced by most people. I can't think of any such unhealthy practices that could conflict with secularly expressed principles of justice. In fact, it would probably only be a religion that practiced human sacrifice, or engaged in practices like handling poisonous snakes, that would conflict with the secular duty to protect human life. Now if your religion practices human sacrifice or something like it, then you and your fellow believers would have a problem in secular society. However, could the practitioner of such a religion be able to enter the social contract with any constitutional democracy in good faith?

For example, historically speaking, the Canadian social contract was originally between English Protestants and French Catholics. That social contract includes, by tacit agreement as it were, transferring to the state the enforcement of the basic principles of justice their respective traditions had already affirmed centuries before there ever was a nation called Canada. Later, that social contract included Jews, and it now seems to include Muslims, Hindus, and Buddhists. That is why I, as a traditional Jew, can be a citizen of Canada in good faith. It is because Canada respects my right of freedom of religion, and because Canada is committed to enforce the basic rules of justice my Jewish tradition requires of any society worthy of the moral loyalty of Jews—indeed the moral loyalty of any rational human being. Thus, neither my freedom to practice Judaism nor my duty to obey the laws of Canada are entitlements from the Canadian state. Instead, both my religious right and my secular duty come from sources that transcend the Canadian state both historically and in principle. But if Canada ever threatens my religious freedom, or abandons its traditional commitment to what I consider to be universal standards of justice, then I would have to ask myself whether I could continue to be a citizen of Canada in good faith.

The Right to Discriminate

Getting back to our paradigmatic case of Marc Hall and his high school prom, we see the full expression of antireligious rhetoric, not so much from Hall himself, but from those who have adopted his case as a cause célèbre for their larger political agenda. Thus I now turn to the statement made at the court hearing by Douglas Elliot, identified in Schmidt's *National Post* article as a "gay-rights [Canadian] Supreme Court veteran." But before looking at Elliot's remarks, we need to briefly distinguish between being homosexual and being "gay." One could say that whereas all gays (and that includes gay women, most of whom prefer the term "lesbian") are practicing homosexuals, not all homosexuals are gay. (I leave out the question concerning those who have persistent homosexual desire but do not practice what are literally homoerotic acts. The question of desire per se is not a moral or political one but rather a psychological or theological one.) There are some practicing homosexuals who simply want to be left to their sexual privacy in peace. They claim what Isaiah Berlin famously called "negative liberty," or what Louis Brandeis called "the right to be let alone."[5] I think most of us, even those of us for whom homosexuality is morally and religiously objectionable, have no quarrel with their claim on our political noninterference in their lives as homosexuals.

Most of us, I think, would look upon sex in private between consenting adults to be no more the business of a secular state than is friendship between consenting adults. And I would include in such negative liberty the right of homosexual persons not to be discriminated against in civil society in terms of such things as hiring and housing. Gays, on the other hand, make their homosexuality a positive political claim. That is, they ask society to actively affirm their sexually constituted way of life. In the case of Marc Hall, Douglas Elliot and other gay activists asked that this social affirmation be required of a religious institution, one whose tradition expressly forbids homosexual activity by its individual members, and even denies any positive encouragement of homosexuality in public.

Douglas Elliot's revealing remarks indicate the depth of the gay quarrel not only with the Catholic Church, but with the whole Judeo-Christian moral tradition (and I would hope, with the Muslim and Hindu traditions as well). Schmidt speaks of Elliot as "mockingly characteriz[ing] the [Catholic school] board's position."[6] He is quoted as parodying the school board as follows: "We have a constitutional right to discriminate, and by God we have a religious duty to discriminate because if we don't discriminate, we won't be true to the Catholic Church."[7] Talk about hate speech! As a Jew, with centuries of experience in having my faith and tradition mocked and ridiculed in public, the Catholic school board has my full sympathy and support. I assume Schmidt is equally sympathetic and supportive of the court's ruling in favor of Marc Hall and against the school board, though, when she concludes, "the judge came down on the side of Marc, ripping apart the board's prudish view of teenage courtship." In other words, it would seem, Marc Hall and Jean-Paul Dummond should be looked upon as tragic victims of traditional prejudice—like Romeo and Juliet, history's most famous teenage lovers.

The use of the word *discrimination* indicates that Douglas Elliot's quarrel is not so much with religion as the worship of a god as much as it is with morality, of which religions, of course, have been the chief promulgators historically. The fact is, morality by definition *discriminates* in the sense of its Latin root *discriminare*, which means "to differentiate." And if morality is looked upon as a system of rules, what we would call *moral law*, then it is well to remember that the Latin word for law—*lex*—probably comes from the verb *ligare*, which means "to bind," as Thomas Aquinas pointed out in his discussion of the concept of law.[8] As such, morality—anybody's morality—differentiates between acts of which the community governed by that moral system approves and acts of which it disapproves. When moral norms can be prudently translated into positive laws—which some of them never can be so translated for political reasons—then moral approval translates into legal endorsement (such as tax benefits for married couples in the United States), and moral disapproval translates into legal penalties (such as the criminal punishment of adults who seduce children into engaging in sexual acts with them). Now I assume Elliot advocates morality in some areas of human life if for no other reason than he is a member of a self-defined "community." Furthermore, as a lawyer, as an officer of the court sworn to uphold the law of the state, he could not very well make a credible argument for absolute anarchy. So it stands to reason that he would not disapprove of discrimination in those areas of life for which his community and his state advocate moral standards. Discrimination, both against certain acts and against those who willingly and regularly practice them, is part of anybody's morality. Just think of how Elliot's community has made "homophobia" an immoral act, which means that anyone who publicly disapproves of homosexuality is to be condemned morally by the members of his community and their heterosexual sympathizers.

Actually, I would say that the only people who are truly "homophobic," that is, those who irrationally fear homosexuality in themselves and others, are those people who commit acts of violence against homosexuals. Nevertheless, I think it can be shown that their motives are neither moral nor religious but psychologically pathological. Most of those whose opposition to homosexuality is moral or religious are so opposed to it because of an existential respect for all human persons and a concern for what is good for them as human persons. We regard homosexuality—and even more so hateful violence—to be bad for human persons. Thus, I think attempts by gay activists to associate acts of violence (like those committed against Matthew Shepard) with our moral or religious opposition to homosexuality are designed to censure moral debate by reducing moral or religious opposition to homosexuality to psychological pathology. I assume gay activists are rational people who have made a moral choice to act homosexually and publicly promote homosexuality, and I respect their right to make their case rationally in public. I ask from them for myself and others who think as I do the same right and the same respect. Declaring one's moral opponents to be mentally ill—which is what anyone who is truly "phobic" is—sounds too much like the antidemocratic logic of the former Soviet regime when it confined many political dissidents to mental hospitals rather than let them engage in rational public debate. It also sounds too much like the old dismissal of homosexuals as simply mentally ill.

Douglas Elliot is not so much opposed to discrimination per se as he is opposed to discrimination against persons whom he thinks deserve not only to be let alone but who deserve to have their sexual practices positively endorsed by their community. Thus, I can only assume that Elliot chose the word "discrimination" more for its emotional effect than for its rational meaning. But who is Douglas Elliot, who I assume is not a Catholic, to tell, whether emotionally or rationally, the Monsignor John Pereyma Catholic School how to conduct its social activities with and for its own students? Haven't the parents of these students freely chosen to send their children to a Catholic school because it is Catholic? Happily, in Ontario, one has a choice of schools to which to send one's child. And judging from my experience with

Jewish schools there especially (but not exclusively), I know that many parents send their children to religious rather than to secular schools precisely because they are convinced that their traditional morality cannot be taught, or even affirmed, in secular schools today, whether public or private. And that is certainly the case as regards sexual morality—the area of morality we all have the toughest time with, especially when we are high schoolers, becoming acutely aware of our sexual nature as maturing human beings.

What Douglas Elliot is really opposed to is not discrimination, neither of certain acts nor those who practice these acts but rather to the persecution of certain acts and those who practice them. Persecution is the irrational act of penalizing members of a community for acts that the community did not prohibit when these particular persons joined the community. Thus, one could argue that when homosexual acts were criminally proscribed in Canada, homosexual persons could not be citizens of the state in good faith. And, in fact, for those citizens for whom the social contract was explicit and not just one of tacit agreement, namely, immigrants to Canada applying for permanent residence or citizenship in Canada, being a homosexual could preclude one from permanent-resident status and from full citizenship. However, since homosexuality has been decriminalized in Canada, it is irrational to deny homosexual Canadians what are civil rights to which all Canadians are entitled. And by the way, I agree with the decriminalization of homosexual acts, not because I think they are now morally acceptable, but because I think it is politically counterproductive to make laws whose enforcement itself is morally problematic. (The criminalization of sexual acts in today's pornographic climate would encourage, even reward, voyeurism, and proliferate professional informers.)

However, members of religious communities have the freedom to join their religious community, knowing full well that it engages in moral discrimination more specific than that of civil society. Thus, in my Orthodox synagogue, for example, men and women are seated in different pews clearly differentiated from each other. Furthermore, the services are conducted by men only. Is that discrimination? No, because the women in the congregation know their status in the religious system governing the synagogue and accept it willingly.

Furthermore, even those women who have joined Jewish congregations where women and men do sit together, and where women do conduct the services, even those congregations certainly "discriminate" against gentiles. That is, even though no synagogue of which I am aware, no matter how Orthodox, would bar a gentile from attending its services, I know of no synagogue in Canada, no matter how liberal, that would allow a gentile to be a member of its congregation or conduct its religious services. Is that "persecution" of gentiles? No, because the criteria of membership and service in the community are known in advance by all its members, and none of them is there under physical duress. Accordingly, if a gentile wishes to be a member of a Jewish congregation, with all its rights and privileges and obligations, then conversion is readily available for him or her once a serious commitment has been made evident to the leaders of the congregation. And moreover, by Jewish religious standards, a coerced conversion is invalid. In other words, as the great twelfth-century Jewish theologian and jurist Maimonides argued, a gentile should not practice Judaism as a gentile but by becoming a Jew.[9] The logic here is hardly unique to Judaism. Surely it operates in any monotheistic religion. Thus, if one wants to take communion in a Catholic church or an Anglican church or a Lutheran church, for example, then he or she should become a Catholic or an Anglican or a Lutheran. Like the Jewish people, these churches are happy to accept converts in their midst.

In any moral community—and religious communities are those having the most discriminating morality—not all acts are acceptable and not all actors are officially recognized. Thus the use of a word like *discrimination*, when its meaning is assumed to be pejorative ipso facto, is a rhetorical red herring. That is, it distracts us from the antireligious agenda that makes Marc Hall a pawn in a much larger battle, of which he and his Catholic parents seem to be naively unaware.

The Antireligious Agenda

It is an old philosophical question whether a coherent moral system needs a theological foundation or not. Philosophically, I am on the side of those who think that a coherent moral system can only be one that is law-like, that is, moral norms cannot be systematically presented except as a body of commandments. As such, I think that a rational person would only obey the commandment of a god as a categorical imperative, which Kant rightly saw to be what distinguishes morality from the exercise of merely utilitarian self-interest.[10] There is no reason to obey the commandment of someone who is merely my equal, let alone my inferior in power and wisdom. A "god" might be minimally defined as a person whose power and wisdom are beyond ordinary human ability, not equal to it and certainly not inferior to it, and not just in degree but in kind. Moreover, that which enables any such person to be designated a god or "divine" is what Anselm most famously called "that which nothing greater can be conceived."[11]

In monotheistic religions like Judaism, Christianity, and Islam, the category of "the divine" has only one member; hence "divinity" and "God" are identical, as in the declaration of the people of Israel at Mount Carmel during Elijah's encounter with the priests of Baal, "the Lord He is God" (1 Kings 18:39). In other words, the questions *what* is divine, and *who* is God have an identical answer. And, since the Hebrew word for "God"—*elohim*—means "authority," one's "god" might well be designated as "the One to whom I listen without qualification." That is why I am convinced that religion and morality cannot be separated in principle. Ultimately, no human being can justifiably command

me to do anything unless that commandment is the implementation of a divine command, however tenuous that connection
might seem to be. That is why I must disobey unjust legal orders on moral grounds and, ultimately, on theological grounds
as well.

Even though my connection of religion and morality is the
subject of much philosophical debate—and thus no one should
be persuaded by my very brief statement of my philosophical
position on the question above—nonetheless, there is a historical connection between religion and morality that is far more
evident than the philosophical one. The fact is that it can be historically demonstrated that everyone who has gotten any systematic morality in his or her life has *received* it from a primal
community. Usually, the initial locus of that primal community
is one's family, but one's family as part of a larger communal
tradition and not just an association created *de novo* by present contract. By "primal community" I mean that human society
which enabled him or her to be born and for whom one would
risk his life, indeed without whom one would not want to live.[12]
Even the norms that come from one's primal community, which
one believes are so universally rational to be universally valid,
even these norms one cannot look upon as his or her original
discovery. Thus, even the most rationally conceived system of
morality cannot act as if it had no cultural or historical anteced-
ents. To use a rabbinic term, the most we can do is look for new
reasons for old norms (*ta'amei ha-mitsvot*).[13]

When one looks to his or her primal community, that is, to
the sources of one's historical identity, it becomes evident, soon-
er for some and later for others, that the identity of this community has been conceived religiously. For Jews and for Christians,
that means one's prime communal identity is to be part of the
elect people of God. Of course, one can always change his or
her historical identity by identifying with another historical culture, however much one's original community might disapprove
of such apostasy. And in a secular democracy, one has the option

to have no historical-cultural identity at all. Nevertheless, those who have opted to have no historical-cultural identity, who have opted simply to be "autonomous individuals," are inevitably unable to resist seeing all their rights become entitlements from the state. That is because none of these rights can be conceived to be ontologically prior to the authority of the state and therefore none of them are essentially outside its control. Furthermore, none of these entitlements are irrevocable. What the state gives the state can always take away. Thus, it would seem that the only right that is ontologically prior to the authority of the state is the religious liberty of the more ancient religious communities and the freedom of individuals to become permanent members of these communities. They alone predate the state and will survive long after the state—any state—will have passed away.

Those who are opposed to the exercise of moral judgment within religious communities understand this historical trajectory very well. That is, they know very well that most people get their morality from religious communities and their historically transmitted traditions. At the bottom of all their protest about "discrimination" is the assumption that sexual behavior, as long as it is not coercive, should have no inherent moral structure at all. Instead, it should be an area of human action for which, as the Talmud describes moral anarchy, "there is no law and there is no judge."[14]

Usually, their means of attack is political. Thus they most often attack the imposition of "religious" morality on a secular polity. They usually attempt this argument by asserting a fundamental difference between rational morality, which is for everybody, and religious morality, which requires religious belief in *a* revelation, thus excluding believers in *another* revelation or *no* revelation. Inevitably, in this view, questions of sexual morality are put in the category of religious morality, something that is "parochial" and thus to be kept within the bounds of one's own religious community. The hope here is that eventually more and more people will see the denial of sexual liberty to be akin to the quaint practices of sectarian groups like the Amish or the Hasidim; that is, practices we might still tolerate, but only from afar. In other words, they are usually careful to separate questions of public morality from the right of religious freedom.

But what we are now seeing in a case like that of *Hall v. the Durham Catholic District School Board* is a new and bolder tactic. The opponents of an inherent sexual morality have now taken their case into the area formerly reserved for religious freedom. That is because they know full well that this is the place where most people get their standards of morally acceptable and morally unacceptable sexual behavior. And they know full well that inevitably these same people bring these moral standards with them into secular society. Furthermore, they know that when these religious people become aware of the political validity of these standards, they simultaneously discover that persons from a variety of other traditions have come to quite similar moral conclusions as themselves. As such, they discover that many of these moral standards are not only revealed but that they are rational as well, that they can be argued for in universal terms. That is why our opponents now realize that their attack should be a direct invasion of the cultural motherland of these views that are so at odds with what in the end is nothing more than a justification for a complete lack of inherent moral standards in the area of human sexuality.

Nevertheless, most people know full well that because of its great complexity, sexuality is the area of human life in greatest need of moral standards. For most people, sexuality is just too important an area of human life to be left to a matter of taste. In the end, the Durham Catholic District School Board has as much right to determine *who* may attend its social activities and *how* he or she may attend them as it has the right to teach Catholic theology in its religion classes as authoritative teaching. Every activity of a Catholic school should be recognizably Catholic, just as every activity of a Jewish school should be recognizably Jewish. And Catholics should not be confined to a moral and political ghetto anymore than Jews or Evangelicals or Muslims should be so confined. Thus the legal assault on the Catholic school board is an assault on the integrity of every religious community in Canada. It should not be left to the final decision of any particular human court.

Keeping the Faith

So far, I have discussed in one way or another the main themes of religious freedom, human dignity, and the public good. But how do we "keep the faith"? And which faith? Surely there are great differences on faith questions: between various Christian churches, between Christians and Jews, and between Christians and Jews and those whose God is not the God of Israel. Nevertheless, not only do we have considerable moral commonality, I dare say there is a commonality of faith among ourselves that is directly connected to our moral concerns. That connection concerns justice. Morality for all of us is the pursuit of a justice whose laws are not of our own making. Moreover, not only is this just law not of our own making, its full and final implementation is also not of our own making. All we can do is to help apply this justice wherever we can do so coherently and effectively, despite all our human limitations. We are not its beginning and we are not its final end. We must only do what we must do somewhere in the middle of the story. As such, our political victories are not final victories and our political defeats are not final defeats. Because of that, we can neither gloat nor despair. We can only hope and attempt to do what is right whenever we are given the opportunity and the privilege to do so by the One who is the beginning and the end of all justice in and for the world. Let us hope that by seeking this justice here and now, we will all be worthy of its final consummation at a time only God's eye has yet seen.[15]

5

God and Human Rights:
A Biblical-Talmudic Perspective

God, Human Rights, and Democracy

The concept of human rights is endemic to democracy. Indeed,its acceptance is what distinguishes a democracy from "ordered brutality," to borrow the words of the leading democratic legal philosopher Ronald Dworkin.[1] To be sure, some democratic theorists have argued that there is an overemphasis on human rights, but that is when human rights are reduced to individual claims on society at the expense of individual responsibilities to society.[2] Nevertheless, it is hard to find any such conservative critic of the overemphasis of human rights who would argue in principle for the value of a societal system that affirmed no human rights at all and only enforced acts that are duties to itself. And as it turns out in fact, human rights seem to be affirmed only in democratic societies. Nondemocratic societies, such as those run according to fascist, communist, or clerical (wrongly called "theocratic") ideologies, are notorious for their denial of any human right that could challenge the absolute authority presumed by those who have power.[3] So, these other forms of society are not only nondemocratic in principle, they are almost always antidemocratic in practice, as evidenced by their contempt for human rights, even their contempt for the *concept* of human rights.

Religious people who affirm the value, even the necessity, of democratic society should be prepared to show how human rights are affirmed by their respective traditions. Religious people should also be prepared to show people from other traditions how their own tradition can provide guidance to these "others" in their concern for human rights, and how the reception of such guidance by no means requires acceptance of the governing authority of one's own tradition. In other words, one needs to argue in a truly universal way and thus not use insights from one's own tradition to proselytize or even engage in any kind of apologetics. One must walk the fine line between triumphalism and obsequiousness. In this context, then, I do not speak *for* the Jewish tradition but, instead, as a philosopher thinking *out of* the Jewish tradition, that is, not as a theologian let alone as a religious jurist (*ba'al halakhah*).

There is a great difference, though, between religious members of a democracy and its secularist members, especially in the ways they affirm human rights and even in the way they determine what some of these rights are. Also, even when religious people and secularists agree about a certain human right in practice, they frequently differ as to who are the actual subjects of this right. By "religious members" of a democracy, I mean those who publicly affirm their relationship with a god (most often, for them, the God) and who assert that their relationship with God has bearing on their political commitments, especially their commitment to human rights. By "secularist members," I mean those who deny that anyone's relationship with God should have political significance. (Such secularists are not necessarily atheists in their private lives, but it seems that most of them whom I know have no god even in their private lives.) The religious members of a democratic society assume that public affirmation of human rights needs an affirmation of God. (But, as we shall see, that "need" is philosophical, not political.) Secularist members of a democratic society deny that such an affirmation of God is needed, let alone desirable.

Religious members of a democratic society should be prepared to publicly argue why their affirmation of human rights needs a prior affirmation of God, and suggest why this need is not just theirs. Nevertheless, they should do this without requiring any such prior affirmation of God from those who do not believe in God as the price of admission to philosophical discourse with believers, especially discourse about human rights in secular society. Indeed, to require any prior religious affirmation for admission to political discourse in civil society would be most undemocratic in any democracy that also affirms religious liberty (which, as I discussed in chapter 3, is the liberty to affirm some religion or to deny any religion at all). Moreover, in debates about the foundations of human rights, religious members of a democratic society need only show why their religious affirmation of human rights provides a stronger foundation for these rights than do the various secularist alternatives, not that these secularist alternatives have no plausibility at all. Secularists, on the other hand, should show why they do not regard a religious affirmation of human rights to be inherently antidemocratic. Indeed, if they do regard such affirmations to be antidemocratic (as some of them certainly have done), then their logic should also lead them to move for outlawing religion in public. But that would be as antidemocratic as requiring citizens in a democracy to have one particular religion or even any religion at all.

Since I am a religious member of a democratic society, I can make only a religious case for human rights in good faith. Secularists should make their own arguments by themselves, and I am always prepared to listen to them carefully since I want to live in peace with them in civil society. Nevertheless, secularists should be able to do so without denying me the right to connect my religious belief to my political advocacy, just as I should be able to do so without denying them their right to connect their nonbelief to their political advocacy. This type of reciprocal respect clearly recognizes that no one comes to political advocacy from nowhere, that all of us, believers and nonbelievers alike, come to our respective political positions from prepolitical commitments.[4] For most people, their prepolitical commitment is religious. Yet there are people whose prepolitical commitment lies elsewhere. It is important for this secularist minority to locate for the rest of us more explicitly just where they are coming from. Religious people, on the other hand, should realize that no human coercion, whether legal or moral, should ever be employed to pressure secularists into making any sort of religious commitment. Thus I do not deny anyone's right to argue his or her affirmation of human rights in public, even when I also think their original reasons for such affirmation are wrong or insufficient. I ask for the same right from those who think my original reasons are wrong or insufficient.

Biblical Precedents

Let us now tentatively define human rights to be those justified claims an individual makes upon the human collective among whom he or she lives, that is, his or her society. And in a society where the moral authority of God is recognized, all such claims are clearly justifiable insofar as they refer to God's moral authority. By "God's moral authority," I mean God as the original source of moral law, and God as the judge who ultimately enforces that moral law.

By "secular society," I mean a society that does not look to any particular historical revelation to justify its political existence and its legal authority. Thus a secular reason is one that does not look to any revelation as its moral source, but that does not mean God cannot be cogently invoked when making a moral or political argument in a secular context. Accordingly, one need not be a secularist to speak and act secularly. One can very much be a religious advocate of secularity; in fact, I think, a better advocate of secularity.

The first illustration of the relation of human rights to God is the statement of an actual biblical norm. "Any widow or orphan you shall not oppress. If you do wrong them, when one of them does complain to Me, I shall listen to his complaint. Then My anger shall burn and I shall kill you by sword; thus your wives will become widows and your sons orphans" (Exod. 22:22–24).[5] Now this clearly refers to an individual who has a legitimate claim on his or her society. The language of scripture indicates that the victim is an individual person: *a* widow *(almanah)* or *an* orphan *(yatom)*. The use of the plural "you" and "your" indicates that it is a collective that is victimizing these individuals who are, no doubt, taken to be the most obvious examples of a larger class of those who are socially and economically vulnerable, and who are usually without powerful advocates on their behalf.[6] The presentation of this norm in the sequence of the biblical narrative, however, seems to assume that the reader is already familiar with the way injustice and its rectification have been described earlier in that narrative.

The language in Exodus is reminiscent of two previous instances of rights violations and their rectifications by God in Genesis. Indeed, it is God whose original rights have been violated in the person of those created in his image, and it is God who will ultimately vindicate the innocent and punish the criminal. The key term is the word for "cry" *(tsa'aqah),* which is the appeal of the innocent victims of crime for justice to be done, both justice for themselves and justice to those who have so victimized them. To whom do they cry for justice, originally and ultimately?

The first example comes from the first rights conflict in the Bible's presentation of human history: the conflict between Cain and Abel, a conflict that led to the first murder. There, an original appeal is made to God to enforce a human right, in this case the human right to have one's murder avenged. Thus God says to Cain immediately after he has murdered his brother Abel, "What you have done! Your brother's blood is crying [*tso'aqim*] to Me from the ground" (Gen. 4:10).[7]

In the Cain and Abel story, Abel has a claim upon Cain: do not kill me! Why? Because God takes personal interest in every human person who has been created in the divine image. In fact, that is very likely what it means to say that all humankind is made to "resemble God" (Gen. 5:1), namely, God and humans are interested in each other insofar as they share some commonality, a commonality not found in God's relations with the rest of creation. "And the Lord God said that humans are like one of us, knowing good and bad" (Gen. 3:22).[8] As such, an assault on any other human being is taken to be an assault on God himself; in fact, one's ultimate reason for assaulting another human being might be because this is the closest one can come to assaulting God. Let it be remembered that Cain was still angry with God for having rejected his sacrifice (Gen. 4:4–7) just before we read that "when they were in the field, Cain rose up against Abel his brother, and killed him" (Gen. 4:8). Killing his brother Abel, whom God had favored, might well have been his attempt to take revenge on God.

Yet the very fact that it is Cain who initiates religion by being the first to offer "a gift to the Lord" (Gen. 4:3) shows that Cain himself surely believed that God takes a personal interest in him and his brother who joined him in this act of worship (the two of whom at that point in history constitute humankind). One brings a gift only when one has an intuition that it will be welcomed, even expected, by the one to whom it is being given. Cain is surely familiar with God when God asks him, "Where is Abel your brother?" (Gen. 4:9). So, because it is assumed that God takes a personal interest in every human person created in his image, we can thereby infer that God prohibits one human from harming another and that God will not allow one who harms someone else to escape retribution for his or her crime. Because of that personal interest, both in the experience of the victim and in the act of the victimizer, God will not allow any crime between human persons to go unnoticed without proper response to the moral situation of both persons so involved, whether victim or assailant.

The difference between the account of Cain and Abel, which we have just examined, and the proscription of injustice against the vulnerable and the promise of divine retribution in Exodus, which was brought as the prescriptive example of God's involvement in human rights, concerns who is the victimizer, not who is the victim. In both accounts the rights of a vulnerable human individual are being violated, whether that victim be one's younger (and presumably weaker) brother, or a widow, or an orphan. But whereas in the Cain and Abel story we have only two individuals—there being no organized society until Cain "builds a city" (Gen. 4:17)—in the Exodus account there is an organized society. It is the society of the Israelites who have just accepted God's offer to be "a holy nation" (Exod. 19:6), which means they were already a nation that was now to become a holy nation especially covenanted with God. The fact that they were already a nation even before being covenanted with God is evidenced by their already having a system of laws by which cases of injustice were being adjudicated. Even before the revelation of the Torah (beginning with the Ten Commandments) at Mount Sinai, a court system was already in place (Exod. 18:20–24).[9] The purpose of that court system was to protect the human rights of those who had been wronged by others.[10]

Since there was no society at the time of Cain and Abel, Abel can only appeal directly to God for justice. There is no one else to avenge his death. In the Exodus account, however, there are two possibilities. One, a victim of crime can appeal to the social collective to enforce his or her God-given right not to be harmed; or two, a victim can appeal directly to God to enforce that same God-given human right.

It seems that a victim would appeal to his or her society for justice when he could be harmed or when he has already been harmed by another individual member of that same society. It also seems that such an appeal to society would be made in a society that considers its prime duty to be the protection of the human rights of its members, first and foremost their right to be protected from injustice and their right to have injustices committed against them by fellow members of that society avenged. A society that recognizes that the rights it is enforcing are unalienable divine endowments rather than its own revocable entitlements will be able to perform its social duty with maximum cogency because it has earned the rightful trust of its members. As such, that society can in good faith call upon its members to "rightly pursue justice" (Deut. 16:20). According to one rabbinic opinion, it is wrong for a victim to appeal directly to God for justice when there is just human authority already present in his or her society.[11] In such a case, God has delegated the immediate enforcement of justice to the authorities in society, who are to act *in loco Dei* because they understand that "justice is God's" (Deut. 1:17; 2 Chron. 19:6). Nevertheless, those having political power may not assume that because of their collective status they are thereby exempt from the moral obligation to do justice to others, which is what God has already required of individual persons. No person, not even an official of society having collective authority, is above God's law or above God's judgment.

But it is unlikely that a victim would appeal to his or her society for justice if the very injustice being committed is being committed by the society itself through its positive laws and public policies. To be sure, if that society is committed to the enforcement of human rights as being mandated by divine law, then it is still possible that the social injustice being committed can be shown to be inconsistent with the fundamental norms of the political-legal system itself. Here internal rectification of the system itself is still possible, at least in principle. Nevertheless, what if those having political and legal power are in fact unwilling to rectify their own unjust victimization of the innocent and the vulnerable? In that case, the cries of the victims of social injustice will fall on deaf ears, the same deaf ears upon which Abel's cry to Cain for justice (before his being murdered by Cain) no doubt fell.[12] One's only recourse, then, is to seek justice from God. Indeed, a victim of injustice at the hands of society ought to complain to God about what has wrongfully been done to him or her rather than sink into political despair.

Belief in the God of justice, the God who is "the Judge of the whole earth" (Gen. 18:25), gives the victims of injustice the assurance that in the ultimate scheme of things they do not have to "settle" for the injustice done to them or to anybody else, that all injustice will be rectified when God "will rightly judge the world" (Ps. 96:13). And it also means that the victims of injustice may not themselves violate the rights of others by cynically assuming that the harm done to them proves that there is no justice ever, for if so, what difference does it make whether one harms someone else or not? Either the victims assume the idea of justice itself is an illusion, or they assume justice is an ideal having no consequences in any real world.[13] In fact, very often the experience of injustice leads its victims to imitate their victimizers by finding their own victims: "Those to whom evil is done, do evil in return," in the memorable words of W. H. Auden.[14]

One can see true opposition to this type of moral or political cynicism in the instruction, "A sojourner you shall not oppress," the reason being given: "because you know what the life of the sojourner is, since you were sojourners in the land of Egypt" (Exod. 23:9). The noun "sojourner" or "resident alien" is used three times here and has three different referents: (1) a gentile individual living in Israel, (2) the state of being a resident alien in general, and (3) the people of Israel who had been resident aliens in Egypt. It is the concept of "resident-alienhood" in general that enables the Israelites to identify with those living under their own rule. So instead of concluding that one may do the evil done to oneself to someone else, scripture concludes that from the negative we derive the positive.[15] From the injustice done to the Israelites by the Egyptians when they were sojourners in their land we learn the justice the Israelites are to do for the sojourner who lives in their land. "There shall be one justice for the sojourner and the native-born" (Lev. 24:22). Neither justice nor the God of justice died in Egypt, or even in Auschwitz.

Both the Egyptians and the Israelites were expected to already know what are the human rights of sojourners in their respective societies. The Israelites are to respect the rights of their sojourners contrary to the way the Egyptians violated the rights of the Israelite sojourners: "What is hateful to you, do not do to someone else," which the Talmud assumes is the fundamental basic moral precept common to both Jews and gentiles.[16] Respect for the right not to be harmed and to be protected by society, and the corresponding duty not to harm but protect the rights of others, are not just a civil right and a civil duty but, rather, a human right and a human duty. Neither the right nor the duty is to be violated anywhere by anyone, whether that individual is functioning individually or collectively.

The situation of human rights is even worse in a society where basic injustice is built into the very political and legal institutions of the society itself. This comes out in the biblical account of the destruction of the cities of Sodom and Gomorrah, whose citizens are described as being "exceedingly wicked and sinful toward the Lord" (Gen. 13:13). Their evil and sinfulness comes to a head when God announces to Abraham that he plans to investigate "the cry [za'aqat] of Sodom and Gomorrah because it is excessive." According to rabbinic interpretation, the "cry" of the two evil cities is not the cry of the citizenry protesting their innocence before the divine Judge. It seems their society had already determined that "there is no law [din] and there is no judge [dayyan]," which is the rabbinic term for practical atheism.[17] The citizens themselves, being beyond any sense of social guilt, would not have known how to protest their innocence. Instead, the cry is the cry of the innocent people who have been persecuted by that very citizenry of Sodom and Gomorrah, a persecution that had been sanctioned by the political and legal institutions of those cities.[18]

The injustice here is more than the work of individual criminals. Were that the case, the officials of that society could be called upon to properly punish those individuals who have violated the laws of that society. Indeed, the injustice here is more than the work of officeholders who have abused their office. One could call attention to the fact that these officeholders are in violation of the laws of that society, even though in that case, there is often no one more powerful than these officeholders to actually call them to task. That is why, in ancient Israel, it took a prophet to remind kings of their violation of God's law that protected the rights of weaker members of their society. One sees that in the prophet Nathan's rebuke of King David for violating the rights of Uriah (2 Sam. 12:7–10), and in the prophet Elijah's rebuke of King Ahab for violating the rights of Naboth (1 Kings 21:17–22). Both Nathan's rebuke and Elijah's rebuke were taken seriously because David and even Ahab were rulers of Israelite societies that still recognized God's law and God's judgment.[19] One can even assume that is why the Israelite prophet Jonah was able to call the people of the gentile city of Nineveh to repentance by commanding them to turn away from "the violence which was in their hands" (Jonah 3:8); this was possible because "the people of Nineveh believed in the God of justice" (Jonah 3:5). Thus one sees that, for the Bible, the seriousness with which the moral admonition of prophets was taken is not something confined to Israel. Israel is not the only nation that considers itself answerable to God's law and God's judgment. Furthermore, prophetic moral admonition itself is not confined to Israel. It does not seem that the people of Nineveh listened to Jonah because he was an Israelite prophet telling them to follow the law of Israel; rather, they listened to him because he reminded them to follow God's law as they knew it from their own national experience.[20]

Nineveh could be saved from its own sins, especially its collective ones, because the people there still recognized God's law within their own tradition. But Sodom and Gomorrah were beyond such salvation since their own tradition had already lost any recognition of a divine law that instituted human rights and specified them. In addition, they had already lost any recognition of divine judgment. In talmudic language, they had collectively forgotten both the moral admonition and the moral penalty.[21] Sending a prophet to admonish them would have been futile. Thus when Lot, the nephew of the prophet Abraham, admonishes the men of Sodom not to violate the strangers who have taken shelter in his house as sojourners, they revile him by reminding him that he himself is "this one who has come to sojourn [and who] is now acting as a judge!" (Gen. 19:9)[22]

Sodom and Gomorrah become, for the Bible, the epitome of social and political depravity that deserves the most severe divine punishment.[23] Their being "exceedingly wicked and sinful toward the Lord" (Gen. 13:13) is primarily their violation of basic human rights, a fundamental breach of morality. If so, why is their sin referred to God? The answer seems to be that "one who reviles the poor despises his Maker" (Prov. 17:5).[24] While one is not to abuse any of God's creatures, it seems that this verse refers to God as the maker of every human, whether male or female, rich or poor, "in his image" (Gen. 1:27; 5:1–2; 9:6). In the case of Sodom and Gomorrah, the violation of human rights is so endemic to the social system itself that there is no longer any recourse to either uncorrupted public officials or the traditions of the society itself. Thus there is only recourse to God himself to destroy the cities that have so fundamentally violated his moral law, the law that irrevocably entitles human beings to dwell in safety anywhere on earth, which God "has created to be a safe dwelling" (Isa. 45:18).

Theological-Political Arguments in a Secular Society

I submit that everything represented above, which is only a small sample of biblical-talmudic discussions of God's connection to human rights, is germane to the great debates about human rights now being conducted in the secular societies of the United States and Canada. The founding document of the American republic, the Declaration of Independence (1776), asserts that all humans "are endowed by their creator with certain unalienable rights." The Canadian Charter of Rights and Responsibilities (1982) asserts, "[w]hereas Canada is founded on principles that recognize the supremacy of God and the rule of law." (My interpretation of "the supremacy of God and the rule of law" is not that these are two separate assertions but, rather, that they are two terms in apposition. That is, *the supremacy of God is the rule of God's law*.[25] That is what "supremacy of God" as distinct from the more vague "existence of God" means.) The separation of church and state asserted in the bill of rights of both nations only means that there is to be no official national religion and that there are to be no religious requirements for citizenship or the holding of public office. It also implies that one cannot make a public argument, intended to bring others into agreement with oneself, whose basic premise is "because the Bible says so." Therefore, in public discussions of matters of law and right, one may not make an argument that presupposes the authority of any particular historical revelation such as the Torah from Sinai, the Sermon on the Mount, or the word of the Koran. But one can certainly quote scripture to illustrate and clarify moral truths that can be argued for rationally rather than just authoritatively. Accordingly, one can definitely make an argument from a divine law that one can show is perceivable by human reason and affirmed in many different traditions, both religious and secular (for example, in English Common Law, which can still be invoked as precedent in American and Canadian courts).

Religious people who understand this fundamental distinction will be able to make very cogent arguments in secular society for human rights, rights which are originally *from* God and finally vindicated *by* God. By so doing, they can "find grace and good favor in the eyes of God and of man" (Prov. 3:4).

6

The Human Rights of the "Other" in Jewish Tradition

Rights and Duties

To speak of a right is to speak of a justified claim made by a weaker party upon a stronger party to either do something for or not do something to the maker of such a justified claim. A right is a claim calling for an appropriate response from the one to whom it has been appropriately made.[1] That right is a human right when it is made because the one making the claim is a human being. My being human, then, is the reason for my claim on someone stronger than myself. A human right, then, is the enunciated desire of one human being to another to help him or her fulfill what can be represented as an authentic need of human nature.[2] Human nature is what is inherent to human being, without which human "being" is either grossly deficient or impossible.

Such a claim is made in a society structured by law, what one could call a "polity" (best designated by the German term *Rechtstaat*). The polity, ultimately in the name of its sovereign, warrants the exercise of a right or claim. Minimally, it is a claim upon a stronger "other" not to harm me; maximally, it is a claim upon a stronger "other" to help me survive, even flourish. When a right or claim is made upon the polity to *let* me do something, it asks the polity to neither impede my doing something *ab initio* nor penalize me *post factum* when I have done what they have allowed me to do. When a right or claim is made upon the polity or upon one of my fellow members of the polity, I am asking for their assistance in doing what they have allowed me to do from the beginning. Here again, the reason for either the claim "to be let alone" (like Isaiah Berlin's "negative liberty") or the positive claim for assistance (what Berlin called a "welfare right") is because I am a human being who needs either to be let alone or to be helped—needs that I can express in desire and articulate in the language of rights.[3]

The polity in which a human right or claim is made is greater than any sovereign "state" in the modern sense. Thus, the assertion of human rights as "natural rights" means that the context of such rights is nothing less than God's governance of universal humanity, whose nature it is to be essentially social.[4] (The Stoics took this Aristotelian notion of human sociality and truly universalized it, seeing humans to be "citizens of the cosmos.")[5] The Bible teaches that humans are essentially related to God, the Creator of the cosmos, insofar as they are "the image of God."[6] That seems to mean (contrary to the ancient Epicureans) that humans are able to generally access God's law, at least as it pertains to their own interhuman relations, and to intuit from such normative experience God's concern for his unique human creatures (even though a truly covenantal relationship with God requires specific historical revelation.) To be human, then, means to have the capacity to be commanded by God, namely, to either exercise a right or dutifully respond to the rights of others, *ultimately* in the name of God.[7] (Historical revelation enables the members of the community to whom God has directly spoken to make such claims and to respond to such claims *directly* in the name of God.)[8] Nevertheless, without an ultimate reference to God, natural rights are meaningless inasmuch as a claim is meaningless without an *authorized claimant* behind it, and only

God as the Creator of humankind could possibly authorize any of their claims.[9]

When a right is justified, it thereby entails a duty on the part of the person to whom the right or claim is justifiably made. There is no right without a correlative duty; there is no duty without a prior right. I take "justice" to be the full correlation of all rights and duties. Thus "injustice" occurs when an appropriate duty is not exercised by one to whom an appropriate right or claim has been made, or when an inappropriate claim is made as the right that, in truth, it is not. God, who authorizes all rights and who correlates the duties appropriate to them, is thus variously called by the Bible: "God, to whom justice belongs" (Deut. 1:17); "God, who does justice on earth" (Ps. 58:12); and "the Lord who justifies us" (Jer. 33:16).

Let me take as a prime example the most basic human right: the right not to be killed. I do this as a Jew here reflecting on the Holocaust, where this most basic human right was denied my people, most brutally, everywhere the genocidal Nazi regime seized power.

If I assert my *human right* not to be killed, that means I am claiming from a would-be assailant that he not kill me—why?—because I am a human being, and because we are both members of a social order called "humanity," where each and every one of us ought to be taken to be the image of God, hence the object of God's direct concern. That social order is more than any particular polity in the world; rather, it is the whole humanly inhabited "civilized" world itself.[10] Accordingly, an assault on me is an affront to the One whose image I am, and who will not allow such an affront to be unknown *ab initio* or go unpunished *post factum*. As God told Cain immediately after he had murdered his brother Abel (Gen. 4:10): "O' what you have done! The blood of your brother cries from the ground [upon which it was shed]," which means that God will not ignore what Cain did to Abel directly and what Cain attempted to do to God himself ultimately. Cain's defense, "I did not know" (Gen. 4:9), can be interpreted

to mean "I did not know this is not to be done!" Yet that defense
is rejected by God; it is a lie on the part of the defendant in this
trial before the divine court. It is not only a lie about his dead
brother's whereabouts; it is a lie about his ignorance of his own
moral obligation not to harm his brother.[11]

One does not simply infer a prohibition from the fact that its
violation is punished. It must be assumed the assailant *already*
knew this prohibition.[12] How did Cain know it? He knew it *because* the very presence of a fellow human being reflects enough
of God himself to evoke reverence.[13] Minimally, the person present makes the *prima facie* claim: "Do not harm me!" Maximally,
the person present makes the prima facie claim: "You shall love
your neighbor as yourself" (Lev. 19:18). That is, the presence of
the human neighbor directly claims the fellow human before
him or her: "Benefit me!" And the ultimate warrant for that
claim is because "I am the Lord," in whose image everyone is
created.[14]

Without this immediate normative recognition of a common
humanity (which needs to be ultimately, if not immediately, justified by reference to divine sovereignty over all humanity), both
on the part of the claimant or right-holder and on the part of the
one claimed or duty-holder, one's cry not to be harmed or one's
cry to be helped would be nothing more than begging. That is,
it would be an arbitrary cry for mercy to an equally arbitrary
source of compassion. The appeal itself is from the emotion or
feeling of the claimant to the emotion or feeling of the one being
claimed. Such compassion, whenever it is requested, is admi-
rable; indeed, when it accompanies a justified claim it testifies
to the importance of that claim. Nevertheless, when the cry for
such compassion is merely made without rational justification, it
is morally insufficient. When there is no reason put forth for either the claim or the response to the claim, one cannot very well
presume that there is any justification for such a claim and why
the other is unjustified when avoiding what is only presumed to
be his or her duty. Hence, in this kind of emotional situation, the

rectitude of one's claim could not be judged according to any law any more than neglecting to respond to that claim could be so judged. Accordingly, when the great second century A.D. rabbi Akibah ben Joseph stated: "Compassion is not to be shown in judgment," he did not mean that the law itself is not concerned with benevolence for those who need it most.[15] Rather, he meant that in the process of adjudication the judge should honor the claim of the person he knows to be justified in his or her claim, not the person the judge *feels* is most deserving of compassion. Indeed, it might well be that the person the judge simply feels is most deserving of compassion has simply appealed to his irrational prejudices, often quite intentionally.

Because my being a human creature gives me the right not to be killed, my would-be assailant has the correlative duty not to kill me. My would-be assailant is the stronger party in this life-threatening situation: he now has the power to kill me. That is either a lethal power I do not possess at all or it is a power my would-be assailant can access faster than I. But, when I am the stronger party in this social situation of pursuer and would-be victim, any rationally governed society would surely support my right to defend myself, even if that requires me to kill my pursuer so that he will not kill me first. In this case, though, as a rights-claimant I am still the weaker party, not in relation to my pursuer whom I have just killed in self-defense, but in relation to the legally structured polity of which I am a member. Since my right of self-defense is my claim upon my society, which is certainly more powerful than I am, my claim upon my society is that it not punish me as a murderer for an act committed in self-defense.

Furthermore, I also have a justifiable claim upon the polity to make known to would-be assailants that my right of self-defense will be honored by the polity, that is, I (or anyone like me) will not be prosecuted for murder in a case of self-defense in which killing a would-be assailant is the only way to prevent him or her from killing me.[16] Conversely, I also have a claim upon the polity to protect me from potential assailants by providing a police force, whose duty it is to make it as unlikely as possible that I will have to defend myself from such an assailant. And the polity has the duty to make known to would-be assailants that if they are successful in any assault upon me (be it murder, rape, or battery) or to my property (be it robbery, theft, or vandalism) and they are apprehended by the police, they will then be prosecuted in a court of law and punished after the fact by a punishment prescribed beforehand. In other words, society has a duty as much as possible to protect me from being a victim of crime, plus a duty to avenge my having been the victim of a crime.[17]

I mention this conceptualization of rights since we need to keep in mind what we mean by use of the term "rights," especially "human rights," which must be taken to be universal and therefore to be prior to the constitution of any particular human polity in the world. Talk of human rights is ubiquitous today; nevertheless, the term is too often used to mean what we infer from what we feel are violations of human rights rather than what the concept of human rights defines. Such emotionally stated inferences, though, frequently make any claim into a right. As such, the very term *rights* loses its definite meaning—and hence its normative force—through the fallacy of generalization. This is not, by the way, a denigration of emotion. Certainly, reasoning about such humanly significant things as rights and justice would be hollow without emotion or passion. (Here I think of Pope Pius XI's great encyclical protesting Nazi injustice, titled *Mit Brennender Sorge,* which might be translated "with burning anxiety.") Rather, emotion should *accompany* the truly important things human reason attempts to comprehend, a point emphasized by both Plato and Aristotle; and emotion is needed to intuit or initially apprehend the very importance of things like rights and justice, thus indicating *that* they are worthy of sustained rational reflection, and worthy of intense practical implementation.[18] But we need reason to tell us *why* rights and justice are of such concern. To substitute reason with emotion is theoretically confused and often leads to practical irresponsibility.

Such theoretical confusion on the part of many liberals makes some conservatives despair of the concept of human rights altogether. Nevertheless, what the concept of rights requires is rational clarification. To obliterate it altogether, though, is either to revert to the raw anarchy of the exercise of political power for its own sake, or to propose irrational duties, since duties can only be justified by their correlation with justifiable rights. Without correlative rights, duties lack any justification, hence any true rationale. Therefore, it is far more intelligent to define what we mean by a right, that is, to justify it, and then to infer from that conceptual definition and justification what violates such a right by not responding to it with the appropriate duty. It is often wiser to infer the negative from the positive than to infer the positive from the negative.

Here is where a religious tradition like Judaism is extremely enlightening. Despite the antireligious prejudices of many liberal and conservative proponents of rights, the concept of rights had been developed in religious traditions like Judaism long before there was a phenomenon like modern secularism. Furthermore, a religious tradition like Judaism is still very much alive, and in its own way, still concerned with the same issues that concern secularist proponents of rights. Indeed, I think it is the task of religious theorists to provide better rationales for human rights than secularists, with their metaphysical blind spot, can possibly do. And I think that a religiously inspired rationale for human rights can be made without requiring acceptance of the particular religion of the person offering such a rationale, or any religion, on the part of those to whom such a rationale is being made.

With this in mind, we can now proceed to the question of how human rights have been understood in the Jewish tradition, and why the question has become so important in recent Jewish experience.

Jewish Powerlessness and Jewish Power

Being politically powerless for most of our history, certainly for almost all of our history in Europe, we Jews have been very much the "other," the weaker party continually having to make a claim on the stronger gentile party for our lives, our property, and our religio-communal liberty. I am convinced that because of that experience of powerlessness, the depths of which occurred during the Holocaust, the ethical philosophy of the most important European Jewish philosopher of the second half of the twentieth century, Emmanuel Levinas, emerged. One cannot understand the poignancy of Levinas's emphasis of the rights of the "other" (*l'autre*), or its continuing influence today, without bearing in mind Levinas's wartime experience as an "other"—the most extreme outsider—that is, a hunted Jew in Nazi-occupied France.[19] Only an "other" can make a moral claim. Only an *other* can assert a right. Levinas is the most philosophically impressive, but by no means the only, post-Holocaust Jewish thinker who has been in the forefront of the movements for universal (or "global" as some like to say) human rights (what some still call "international" rights). The experience of the Holocaust has made Jews effective advocates for universal human rights, and indeed, many non-Jewish advocates for universal human rights have invoked the experience of the Jews as the prime example of what happens when universal human rights are violated or when whole segments of humanity are denied the status such rights presuppose as their subject. Only beings taken to be human unequivocally are the bearers of unequivocal human rights.

Some Jewish thinkers, though, have drawn metaphysical conclusions from the historical situation of victimhood that has been the lot of Jews for most of our history, especially for most of our recent history. They have attempted to see victimhood as being endemic to the perennial condition of the Jews, namely, that Jews are always and always to be the weaker party in any political relationship in the world, always the hunted one, always the ones selected for annihilation.[20] When illustrated by the Holocaust, this becomes the notion that the Jews are always to be in mortal danger, and as such, our only task in the world is continually to assert our right to life in the face of a world whose nations are always the stronger party: the party always to be claimed by the Jews, but never to make any claims upon the Jews.

This type of metaphysical characterization of the Jews is understandable, but it is, nonetheless, unfortunate, both theologically and ethically. It is unfortunate theologically because it turns the Jewish doctrine of the election of Israel into a notion of "selection," where oppressors continually seek us out for death rather than the Universal God seeking us out for life—both in this world and in the world to come. And it is unfortunate ethically because it impedes the development of a Jewish doctrine of the responsibilities of power over other people, a power we now have after the establishment of the State of Israel in 1948, and especially after 1967, when Jews have had power over a number of non-Jews almost equal to the number of Jewish Israelis. In other words, Jews need to think of "otherness" in new ways, both theologically and ethically.

Theologically, Jews need to think of ourselves not so much as the weaker *other* in relation to the nations of the world but rather, as the weaker *other* whom God elects for the covenantal relationship.[21] This election gives us our true destiny in this world and beyond. And this election, which makes us the covenantal partners of God, gives us far greater control over our lives in this world than the view that we are the objects of the arbitrary selection of our very evil persecutors and murderers. Ethically, Jews need to think very carefully about what it means not to be "the other" but, rather, what it means to be faced by a non-Jewish "other," where we have political power far greater than whatever political power this non-Jewish other has over us.[22]

Although I am a Jew and a Zionist (meaning I support my people's establishment of a Jewish state in the land of Israel),

I am not an Israeli citizen. As such, it is not for me to discuss, let alone evaluate, the legal and political details of the way the State of Israel is dealing with the issue of non-Jewish *others* in her midst. Nevertheless, if ethics (which, as Aristotle pointed out, is not separate from politics, when both are broadly and deeply conceived) and theology are integrally intertwined in Judaism, then the theologically charged Jewish tradition can provide some ethical guidance (if not actual political governance—as yet) when Jews, and not just Israeli Jews, ponder this question.

Happily, the Jewish tradition, particularly in the discussions in the Talmud and its commentaries, is not altogether silent on the question of the proper exercise of Jewish power over non-Jewish subjects. Yet most, if not all, of these discussions are more speculative than immediately normative since they do not invoke actual cases (of which there were none, aside from the institution of slavery, which no one interested in human rights today could possibly want to revive and no one in the Jewish tradition need revive). Now, one could see these discussions as having little ethical influence since they were, in fact, the speculations of those *under* the power of others *imagining* what it is like to have power *over* others. However, the very disconnection of these discussions from actual cases might well give these discussions more ethical influence precisely because we cannot reduce them to a particular set of historical circumstances. These kinds of discussions are the kind of theorizing that can lead to intelligent praxis.[23]

The Resident-Alien from Rabbinic Sources

One sees the speculative-political treatment of the non-Jewish other best formulated in the rabbinic discussions of what the rabbis called the *ger toshav,* usually rendered into English as "resident alien." Now the first thing to remember about the *ger toshav* is that rabbinic discussions of him (or her) are admittedly anachronistic. The specific right of the *ger toshav* to permanent domicile in the land of Israel is restricted by the Talmud to the time when all twelve tribes of Israel actually lived in the land according to the prescribed tribal boundaries. But that condition has not been in effect since as early as the destruction of the Northern Kingdom of Israel (Samaria) in 721 B.C.[24] What his or her right to domicile in the land of Israel under less-than-full Israelite presence and rule is to be is a debated question among later rabbis.[25] Hence the discussions of the *ger toshav* are, in fact, imaginative descriptions of what *might have* been in the past occasioned for the sake of what *might be* in the foreseeable (pre-messianic) future, that is, when Jews regain political control of the land of Israel in part or in full.

A gentile is to become a *ger toshav* in one of two ways. The first way is when an individual gentile appeals for a type of citizenship in a Jewish polity. The second way is when a Jewish polity conquers a group of non-Jews.

Concerning the first way, we read:

> Who is a *ger toshav?* [He is] whoever takes upon himself, before an authorized Jewish tribunal [*sheloshah haverim*] as obligatory not to engage in idolatrous worship [*avodah zarah*]: in the words of Rabbi Meir. But the Sages say he is whoever takes upon himself as obligatory the seven commandments [*sheva mitsvot*] the Noahides took upon themselves as obligatory. Other Sages say . . . Who is a *ger toshav?* This is an alien [*ger*] . . . who takes upon himself as obligatory all the commandments stated in the Torah, except the prohibition of eating animals that died (rather than having been properly slaughtered by Jews [*nevelot*]).[26]

As far as the actual codification of the law is concerned, the law is to be according to the view of the sages.[27] It alone assigns a definite body of law to the *ger toshav*.

The author of the text just quoted assumes that his readers already know what the "Noahide" commandments are. Also, he assumes that these commandments have been known at least since the time of Noah and his descendants who, having been the only humans to survive the flood, are themselves synonymous with humankind itself, that is, reconstituted humankind. The seven Noahide commandments (what some now call "Noahide law") are one (positive) prescription and six (negative) proscriptions: (1) to establish courts of law; (2) not to blaspheme; (3) not to practice idolatrous worship; (4) not to engage in incest, adultery, homosexuality, and bestiality; (5) not to shed innocent blood; (6) not to rob; and (7) not to eat a limb torn from a living animal.[28]

On the question of the origin of the Noahide commandments, scholars are divided. Some of them clearly see Noahide law as Jewish law that the Jewish tradition has *posited* for the gentiles ruled by Jews or who have been influenced by Judaism.[29] Yet the only such commandment that seems to be directly derived from a positive biblical statute is the prohibition of eating a limb torn from a living animal. ("Surely meat with its life-blood still in it, you shall not eat"—Gen. 9:4.) All the rest of the commandments can only be inferred from biblical texts, texts that *describe* their general acceptance rather than texts that specifically *prescribe* the specific norm to be done. This fact no doubt has led other Jewish scholars to see Noahide law to be a Jewishly recognized version of natural law.[30] (In other words, the *general* description of the prevalence of these norms is a description of their *universal* normative validity, which human reason can *constitute*.) Indeed, all the Noahide commandments—with perhaps the exception of the torn limb commandment—seem to be norms that other traditions besides Judaism *reconfirm,* rather than assert that they have either invented these norms themselves or received them de novo in a special historical revelation directly from God. (And perhaps one could see the law of the torn limb to be an example of a more general proscription of cruelty to animals, what the Talmud calls *tsa'ar ba'alei hayyim*.)[31]

This would explain how the institution of the *ger toshav* presupposes the reality of the universal Noahide, rather than taking the two to be synonymous. As such, it would also explain how Judaism could possibly influence non-Jews it has neither the likelihood nor even the desire to actually rule through the exercise of Jewish political power over them. In other words, there *were* Noahides *before* anyone could be deemed a *ger toshav,* and there *are* Noahides *after* anyone could be literally deemed a *ger toshav* (at least in the sense of someone allowed permanent residence in the land of Israel when either all twelve tribes of Israel are still living thereon or some of the tribes regain political control therein). That being the case, it is possible within a political system structured by traditional Jewish law to envision a situation in which there *could be* someone like the *ger toshav.*[32] Moreover, Noahide law could also be a guide for Jewish political activity in the Diaspora, in those societies where Jews equally *participate* in the political and legal processes. In fact, even in medieval societies where Jews did not have political and legal equality as full citizens, Noahide law still provided a powerful heuristic device for their moral and theological judgment of the Christians and Muslims they either lived among or lived under as to whether or not they could be respected by Jews. So, one can see the recognition of the acceptance of Noahide law—whatever it is actually called—to be a Jewish recognition of the exercise of human rights by whole communities of the non-Jewish "others."[33]

The Noahide prohibitions of bloodshed, sexual immorality, and robbery could definitely be considered what we would call today "civil rights," not so much because they are invented by the polity (*civitas*), but because they are the personal rights that need to be enforced in any civilly decent society. And here we get back to the earlier question of the correlation of rights and duties.

Taking the idea of Noahide law to be a Jewish version of the idea of natural law, and taking natural law or natural justice to be the proper correlation of duties with the rights these duties presuppose, one should then ask why the *ger toshav* is required to reconfirm prior duties. Shouldn't the *ger toshav* be exercising prima facie rights or claims? In other words, shouldn't the Jewish tribunal before whom a gentile is applying to become a *ger toshav* first provide a bill of rights for this applicant for secure, even if second-class, citizenship in a Jewish state? Indeed, the fact that the Jewish tradition presents duties rather than rights prima facie, the fact that there are *commandments* (both for Jews and for gentiles), seems to indicate that Judaism is a system of duties rather than a system of rights. So why then are duties presented first, whereas we can only infer from them what rights lie behind them?

Here is where a phenomenology of "normativity"—as the experience of living under law—is helpful. Our first experience of living under law is our childhood experience of being *ordered* by our parents. When we children were cooperative, wanting to please our parents, they *asked* us to do certain things and to refrain from doing others. When we were not cooperative, not wanting to please our parents, they *commanded* us to do certain things and refrain from doing others. Later on in life, if we had good parents, we learned that what they wanted us to do or not do was beneficial to us: *for our own good* as well as *for their good*. We needed to fulfill our childish needs to grow up into the world and they needed to fulfill their adult needs to help us do so. But at the time we were first aware of being ordered, our prime concern was to respond to our parents' need for us to cooperate with them in the domestic work of maintaining family life. Only after being aware of this family *order* and remembering its experience were we able to make intelligent, justifiable claims on others. (Without such intelligible experience, we could only shriek like animals.) In other words, we must be claimed before we can properly claim, before we can properly express a claim and exercise the justified right it is.[34] Without being able to understand the difference between a justified and an unjustified claim made *upon* us, we could not make a justifiable claim and refrain from making an unjustifiable claim upon others. We need to *be claimed* before we *can claim;* we need to be known by an other before we can truly know an other. And following our analysis of this primary psychological experience, we often see how children who were either overindulged or neglected by bad parents frequently make bad fellow citizens. Those who have been overindulged regard their every desire as a right requiring no rational justification; those who have been neglected don't even bother with rights talk at all, simply taking (sometimes with psychopathic cunning) what they feel they have been deprived of.

When it comes to the actual rights the *ger toshav* can claim from a Jewish polity, it can only be assumed that these rights correlate with the duties they have accepted or reconfirmed during the procedure before a Jewish tribunal that gave them the status of *ger toshav.* One can only assume that the biblical mandate "one law there shall be, both for the sojourner and for the native-born" (Lev. 24:23) means that the civil and criminal rights *and* the civil and criminal duties of the resident-alien are similar (if not altogether identical) to those of the native-born Jew, duties which, as we have seen, presuppose correlative rights. Surely no gentile would possibly become a *ger toshav* in good faith unless he or she were assured that as a *ger toshav* he or she could be subject to the protection of their rights by the law as much as they would be subject to the imposition of their duties by the law.[35] And along these lines, there is the duty of Jews to be beneficial to gentiles living among them for the "sake of peace" (*mipnei darkhei shalom*), peace which we can see to be the rights these gentiles truly have.[36] Doesn't the peace of a Jewish polity, with both Jewish and gentile citizens, require at least as much symmetry between duties and the rights they presuppose in order to be rational?

A Community of Resident-Aliens

The issue of peace between Jews and non-Jews over whom Jews have or could have power leads us to consider a situation where the Noahide commandment to establish courts of law might actually be put into practice. That situation is when a Jewish polity conquers an entire gentile community. Summarizing and reinterpreting several disparate rabbinic sources, Maimonides, the most philosophically systematic of the codifiers of Jewish law, states:

> And so it is with a non-Jewish city that has made peace with us [she-hishleemah], a covenant [berit] is not to be made with them until they renounce idolatry and destroy all its shrines and accept the rest of the commandments the Noahides have been commanded. . . . And so did Moses our Master command us by the word of God [mi-pi ha-gevurah] to force [la-kof] all the inhabitants of the world to accept the commandments the Noahides have been commanded. . . . Wherever this obtains [be-khol maqom], whoever accepts them [the Noahide commandments] is called a ger toshav.[37]

But the question remains: who is to enforce the Noahide law this *community* of gentiles has accepted and to adjudicate their cases according to this law—the Jewish conquerors or the gentile community themselves? In other words, is this law only *for* the gentile community or is it also *of* this community? That is, is it their law as its *subjects* or is it their law as its *judges* as well? (Being divine law, as is Jewish law for Jews, this Noahide law is not made by its gentile subjects anymore than Jewish law is made by its Jewish subjects for whom and of whom that law surely obtains.)

The liberty of the community of the *ger toshav* is asserted by the great Spanish-Jewish theologian and jurist Moses Nahmanides of Gerona, who writes:

> In my opinion, the obligation of adjudication [*ha-dinin*] that was assigned to the Noahides in their seven commandments required that they not only place judges in every district, but He [God] commanded [too] concerning such matters as stealing and cheating . . . just like the obligation of adjudication that the Jews were commanded.[38]

So Nahmanides sees the legal independence of the subjugated gentile community to be both general and specific. At the general level, it comes quite close to granting this community enough sovereignty to become, for all intents and purposes, a polity per se.[39] (But the question of military independence, which would be more than having its own police force, is unclear in what might be seen as this more "pluralistic" view of the community of the *ger toshav*.)

So far, then, we have seen how a *ger toshav* system could enforce four of the seven Noahide commandments, those that pertain to interhuman relations. And they seem to be consistent with what many other belief systems have regarded to be essential human rights. In fact, the great German-Jewish philosopher Hermann Cohen impressively argued that the Jewish institution of the *ger tohav* could be viewed as a forecast of citizenship in a secular polity.[40] Cohen built on the point that, at least according to Maimonides, the *ger toshav* is not required to convert to Judaism at all, nor should he or she even be seen as someone in the process of eventual conversion to Judaism.[41] A secular polity is one where, minimally, no one is required to convert to any religion to be a full participant in the civil life of the polity. But what about the more "religious" prohibitions: those of blasphemy and the worship of "other gods"?

Religious Tolerance

The prohibition of blasphemy, that is, cursing God, could very well be interpreted as the prohibition of what is becoming known as "hate speech."[42] In this case, that would mean the prohibition of any speech that seriously denigrates the God worshiped by monotheists. But that does not require anyone to actually affirm this God. So even blaspheming atheists are not so much cursing a god they do not believe exists as they are deliberately offending the people who do believe in this God. So, for example, militantly atheistic talk, which is always talk *against* God, is being heard more and more in public.

In other words, it would seem that one can be an atheist in such a Jewishly authorized polity (or its satellite, broadly conceived) as long as one's atheism is not so militant that it entails blasphemy. And as we shall soon see, if Christians and Muslims are taken to be worshipers of the same God as the Jews worship, then blasphemous speech against either Christianity (think of the growing ridicule and denunciation of Christianity by so many otherwise "liberal" people in the West) or Islam (think of the "Salman Rushdie affair") would need to be proscribed anywhere Jewish believers could exercise political power.

But the most difficult Noahide commandment to represent in a modern system of human rights is the prohibition of the worship of "other gods." It seems to imply that a polity must have an official religion and that any competitors of that official religion be outlawed. However, we need to examine this question more carefully.

Even where there is an official religion, such a religion need only outlaw every other religion within the polity if it also assumes that these other religions are the worship of false gods. If so, then the adherents of these other religions, with their worshipful affirmation of false gods, are guilty of public deception, something akin to what we would now call "perjury." But that assumes that the official religion, in this case Judaism as the official religion of a truly Jewish polity, sees itself as having a monopoly on the One and Only God. In this view, a person is either a Jewish monotheist or a gentile polytheist. As for Noahides, it would seem that they are quasi-Jews, that is, they are

Jewish enough not to be polytheists anymore but gentile enough not to adhere to the full Jewish law as yet. (This, by the way, might very well have been the theological-political situation of "sojourners"—*gerim*—in days before the destruction of the First Temple.)[43]

That type of neat distinction worked fairly well until Jews had to deal with Christianity and Islam, both of which assert that they worship the One and Only God, the same God the Jews have already been worshiping all along. Are they consciously lying? Or are they deluding themselves and others? Must Christians and Muslims living under Jewish rule have to defer to the moral authority of Judaism for themselves?

In the case of Islam, almost all Jewish theologians and jurists have regarded it to be a valid monotheism. But in the case of Christianity, due to the doctrine of the Trinity especially, which seems to compromise the oneness of God with the concept of a "triune" God, there have been many Jewish theologians and jurists who have regarded it to be polytheistic and thus "strange worship" (*avodah zarah*), namely, "strange" or "forbidden" even to gentiles.[44] Nevertheless, there is enough solid Jewish opinion, both legal and theological, that assumes that the three *persons* of the Trinity function something like *attributes* of the One and Only God. If so, then Christianity need not be deemed forbidden "strange worship," at least not for its own gentile adherents.[45]

This type of official tolerance of Christianity and Islam might well be politically sufficient since it is hard to imagine any significant group of, let us say, African or Asian polytheists living under Jewish political control of any kind, let alone the political control of religious Jews in the land of Israel. Nevertheless, this still implies the kind of religious imperialism, where the dominating party *allows* the dominated party only to have a religion that the dominating power can regard either as a potential form of itself or a diluted form of itself.

However, let us adopt the view that the weaker gentile community, that of the *ger toshav*, basically runs its own judicial affairs according to what can be recognized as Noahide law, at least in principle. That is something Noahide law, because of its very generality, lends itself to. That would also mean the Noahide prohibition of polytheism and idolatry would be something the gentile authorities themselves would interpret in theory and apply in practice. So, for example, many religions called "polytheisms" by monotheists actually affirm one chief God and regard other, lesser deities to be that chief God's intermediaries. And as in much of ancient Greek polytheism, law is seen as having the ultimate warrant of that chief God.[46] Moreover, because of this judicial independence, involving the power to interpret and reinterpret norms held in common with the Jewish community, a *ger toshav* or "Noahide gentile" (*ben Noah*) would enjoy more religious and political freedom living *collectively* within a gentile polity, recognized but not administered by a Jewish polity, than he or she would have living as an *individual* in a Jewish polity administered by Jews, where all norms, including those applying to gentiles, would be interpreted by Jews according to traditional Jewish criteria.

Conclusion

When examined carefully, the Jewish tradition teaches rights that could be recognized by modern rights proponents. Nevertheless, the Jewish tradition does not endorse many of those rights promoted by modern liberals in recent years. The Jewish tradition does not recognize it to be anyone's right, for example, to have an abortion for anything less than to save the mother's life, or to have any sexual liaison recognized by the state as a marriage, or to be allowed or even assisted to end one's own life. That parting of ways over human rights is, I suspect, the result of a profound metaphysical difference between religious Jews and Christians (and, it now seems, Muslims as well) and secularists who, even if not atheists in private, deny God has any place in the public sphere and the moral law that must necessarily obtain there. That the earth is our dwelling place because God has placed his human creatures here to protect and nurture our lives as familial, communal, and divinely related beings—this biblical teaching, which the best of classical Greek philosophy partially enhances, is the root of all human rights and duties. Like all good roots, it supports the branches that draw their nurture from it, but it rejects those branches which if grafted on would weaken, if not poison, its continuing creative power.

7

Law: Religious or Secular?

Law: Ordinary and Extraordinary

All great legal debates are not about what the law is, but about why there is law altogether and what that law is to be. Such debates are extraordinary, not because they concern what is more unusual or even more bizarre than the subject matter of ordinary legal debates, but in the sense that they directly question the foundations of the law in a way these foundations are not questioned ordinarily. A legal conclusion in such extraordinary debates will not soon be relegated to the historical sidelines as something peripheral. Such a legal conclusion will quickly become the center of much future discussion and deliberation. It will become precedent to be cited again and again. When such debates actually reach the courts, we call the way they have been decided "landmark" decisions. We also frequently use the term "landmark" when a legislature decides such a debate by making a new law to resolve it.

It is the business of ordinary legal debate to decide under which specific rule of law a particular case is subsumed. In ordinary legal debate, such reasoning simply takes what seems to be the proper specification prima facie and applies it to make the conclusion of the law the conclusion of the case. The underlying moral premises of this law, let alone law itself, need not be considered. In fact, much of the ordinary business of law requires this simple type of syllogistic reasoning in which the premises of the deduction are not critically examined. Judgment here is specific, not generic. In most cases, the stability of the legal system itself needs what is readily at hand, either a law on the books or a ruling from a similar case already decided. Ordinarily, questions of the foundations of the law need to be bracketed for reasons of efficiency. Indeed, that is the moral premise of ordinary legal decision making: we are to invoke no principles deeper than what the case before us calls for so as to avoid seemingly endless philosophical discussion. In ordinary cases, such protracted discussion would unduly delay the delivery of justice.[1]

Conversely, it is the business of extraordinary legal debate to decide why a specific law is sufficient to bring justice to a particular case, or why that specific law is insufficient to do so. Such extraordinary judgment is exercised, more often than not, when a decision of a lower court is sent to a higher court on appeal. In such extraordinary debate, two types of extraordinary judgment are called for. When the higher court confirms the ruling of a lower court, the judges must give a new and better reason for the law first applied to the case in the lower court. When the higher court overturns the decision of a lower court on a point of law rather than on a point of fact, the judges need to show why this is so, that is, why another rule of law is more appropriate to the case before them. That too involves giving a new and better reason for the law now deemed more appropriate. On this level, surely something philosophical is required of our jurists, those who are called upon to decide such cases in our highest courts. Whether we get good or bad law from them depends on their philosophical ability as well as on their commitment to justice.

When such extraordinary debate is conducted by legislators, it seems to be due to the recognition that no rule within the existing legal system is sufficient to bring justice to a whole class of cases calling for judgment. That is why a new law is called for.

The difference between good and bad legislation is whether or not the reasons for the new law are true or false. Here, foundations must be considered. Legislation should always deal with what is extraordinary since what is ordinary is already covered by existing law. That is why in the United States and in Canada, where there are written constitutions, all legislation is subject to judicial review by the supreme court of the country. If the new law violates the constitution, then it is to be nullified inasmuch as new law must be consistent with the "old" constitution, even if not directly derived from it. In such cases, it is inevitable that the question before the supreme court will involve consideration of the foundations of the law in one way or another.

Unfortunately, though, there is less remedy for the making of superfluous laws by legislatures, which themselves cannot be overturned inasmuch as they are not unconstitutional. That seems to happen when legislators become professionals in their job, having to convince their constituents they are really doing something "significant" while in office. Our frequently unintelligible tax codes seem to be a prime example of this making of laws without end. But the making of too many new laws seems to emphasize the extraordinary at the expense of the ordinary, thus threatening the stability of the legal system as a whole. That can only lead to a lessening of respect for the rule of law per se. It borders on dangerous sensationalism. When there is confidence in the stability of the legal system, truly innovative legislation should be extraordinary—exceptional—for the sake of preserving the ordinary, which is the locus of most of our justice. Nevertheless, avoidance of the deep judgment required in hard cases, by refusing to recognize their extraordinary status, threatens to leave the system of law without rational foundations at all. Surely, these foundations need to be shown when the justice of the system itself is called into question on these rare, truly significant occasions.

Legislation and extraordinary adjudication have much in common, so much so in fact that we now have debates about where the line between adjudication and legislation actually lies. This is an important question for debate in a constitutional democracy since the de facto usurpation of legislative authority by the courts seems to lead to an oligarchy of judges (which is antidemocratic), and the usurpation of judicial authority by legislators seems to lead to basic instability in the coherence of the legal system over time by its de facto elimination of the priority of the old laws (which is anticonstitutional). We have to very carefully choose which cases are extraordinarily important enough to warrant explicit discussion of the foundations of the law itself, and where the best place for that discussion is: the courts or the legislatures.

Religion in the Law

There is no debate in our society today that is more important than the debate over the role of religion in a constitutional democracy. Religion has become a matter of extraordinary legal debate indeed. Like all great moral questions, it has inevitably come before both the courts and the legislatures. In both places, though, questions pertaining to religion have proven to be uncomfortably difficult to simply subsume under ordinary legal rules or even to make new, intelligent rules pertaining to them. Thus the record of both the courts and the legislatures concerning religious matters is quite erratic because most of our judges and most of our legislators (and their clerks and aides) do not seem to be philosophically reflective enough to deal with the moral issues that are unavoidable whenever religion is at the center of a serious discussion. Also, many of them have very little factual knowledge about religions, let alone much experience in any kind of religious life.

In a democracy, when judges and legislators are not well informed on an issue, they should seek the counsel of citizens who are better informed to help them make rational decisions in such matters. In fact, one could see it as both the democratic right and duty of those citizens who have some counsel for those in authority to offer it whether solicited or not, if for no other reason than as citizens they too will be affected by jurisprudence or legislation in this area, either for good or for ill.

Too often, the issue of law and religion has been limited to questions of the practice of religious rituals in public. We are used to debates about uttering prayers at public events, or the display of religious scenes on public property, or public aid to parochial schools, or the wearing of religious costumes by men and women in the military, or those citizens who may be exempted from certain public duties because of prior religious duties. Here the question seems to revolve around the issue of whether the legal permission of such religious activity in the public square implies the public endorsement of one religion at the expense of all the others, and at the expense of those who have no religion at all and do not want one.

Although the legal importance of such questions should not be underestimated, the questions do not really deal with the essential philosophical issue of religion in the law of our Western democracies. That question is not how law deals with religious institutions and practices within a realm already secular. It is much more fundamental: can anyone represent religion to be the basis of the rule of law in a constitutional democracy that defines itself as a secular polity? It is clear that in a secular polity, where a specific religious affiliation cannot be a prerequisite of full citizenship, one could not make a public argument to every other citizen that the legitimacy of the state and its law is based on the authority of one's own historical religion, with its full set of institutions and practices. That is because all of this is rooted in a unique revelation and developed in the tradition of a community who has accepted that unique revelation forever. But not everyone in the society is a member of that community or wants to be a member. Hence, acceding to any such specific religious argument would require religious conversion as its logical conclusion. Nevertheless, does that also rule out, *ab initio*, cogently deriving that secular legitimacy from a religious commitment that sees itself as being distinct from the acceptance of the full set of institutions and practices of a specific historical religion? In other words, must the legitimization of a secular—that is, nonsectarian—polity be made from purely secularist grounds or not? Must the legitimization of the polity itself necessarily require atheism de facto if not de jure? Can one have religious reasons for the legitimacy of the secular polity that do not presuppose conversion to (or reconfirmation of) a traditional religious community? Moreover, where does this question most acutely arise politically?

The great moral issues—being of such political import that they quickly find their way into legal debate, such issues as abortion, capital punishment, euthanasia, and who may enter civil marriage, among others—all of these questions are of far greater political import than questions of public displays of religion by private citizens. They are questions that are directly involved in what James Davison Hunter has called "culture wars" (an English version of the older German term *Kulturkampf*).[2] The sides in these culture wars are not to be described by the usual differentiations between "liberals" and "conservatives." They go far deeper than that and they often crisscross over these rather simplistic demarcations. I submit that all of these great questions at the center of our legal-political-moral debates, if not yet our wars, can be reduced to one great question: *does a person's moral adherence to a body of law require a god or not?* Could there be a source of the law itself (the *Grundnorm* in Hans Kelsen's important term) other than a god?[3] In one way or another, how a person answers this great question will determine how he or she answers all the great moral questions that are both debated in public forums and are before the courts and the legislatures. Since all great moral questions are questions of justice, and since justice is the political norm per se, as Aristotle insisted, it is inevitable that great moral questions have immediate legal significance.[4]

The moral-legal debate over religion is deeper than just the question of the practical coexistence of religious practices and secularity inasmuch as most religious people are now democratic enough to reject any notion of governmental coercion in the area of religious affiliation and practice (what we would now call "theocracy").[5] As such, they can tolerate those who are "secularists," those without any religion, just as they can tolerate those having a religion different from their own. And most secularists are still democratic enough not to advocate outlawing religion (as has been the case under communist regimes). As such, they can tolerate those who are religious. After all, if democracy means recognizing the religious rights of minorities, certainly it means recognizing the religious rights of the majority. Most immediately, that means the right to practice one's religion in public. (The fact is that the majority of citizens in the United States and Canada have some public religious affiliation, and even more of them publicly profess belief in some god.)[6]

Nevertheless, there is more to one's religion than that; it also has a body of moral teachings. Hence, does a person have the right to base adherence to the laws of the polity on his or her religious or moral principles? Unlike the right to openly practice one's own religious rites, which can easily be tolerated as part of one's right to an individual "lifestyle," basing one's public moral stance on religious grounds seems to make a claim on everyone in the society. When the question of religion reaches this necessarily public level, even many secularists who are usually tolerant of religion become quite fearful because religion seems to be making a requirement of them, and without their consent. This fear is most often expressed by such words as, "Who are you to impose your religious morality on society?" More crudely, it is expressed as, "Who are you to shove your religion down my throat?" As Kant best taught us, the logic of any moral argument must be capable of being universalizable, that is, directed to everyone without exception.[7]

At this philosophical level, which is not just a question of theory but which is also embedded in extraordinary legal questions, we finally get to what might well be the most important question any human being ever asked: is there God? Here the options seem to be mutually exclusive. Despite the attempt to create a neutral position called "agnosticism," one can show that agnostics are actually timid atheists, those who have not yet taken moral responsibility for their contrary stance regarding God. Thus I am reminded of the time I asked the president of a leading society of atheists what the difference between an atheist and an agnostic is, and he said, "Guts."

Since the connection between God and laws has been constant throughout most of human history, the question of God has inevitably become the question of what is one's basis of moral authority. It is hard to imagine a god who does not command. A normatively neutral god would be functioning at a level of human concern too shallow for people to take upon themselves the type of existential vulnerability invoking such a weighty name as "God" necessarily involves.[8] Even nonbelievers will still use the name *God* for superlative reasons, such as questioning someone's moral authority by asking, "who do you think you are—God?" (Indeed, the most general name for "God" in the Bible is *elohim,* which means "authority": first divine, then human.[9] I shall return to this point later.) The type of atheism that undergirds authentic secularism, by its inevitably vehement denial of any god, is just as concerned with the connection of religion and morality as are religious people. Authentic secularists know very well where the essential question lies, and why the stakes are so high in anyone's answer to it.

The answer to the question of whether your adherence to a body of law requires a god or not is not something where tolerance of principle can be cogently argued, however civil one might want to act toward those holding different principles. There are very good moral reasons for such tolerance of opinion when such argument takes place in a democracy, but at the level of principle more decisive commitment is called for. Discursive pluralism need not lead to epistemological pluralism, let alone ontological pluralism. Truth is a greater issue than prudence. Indeed, the cause of truth itself requires that there be enough social pluralism to enable prudential persuasion rather than co-ercion to be one's modus operandi in public discourse. Anything more than that, however, presupposes the epistemological dead end of relativism and the ontological dead end of nihilism.

At the most theoretical level, on the one hand, we have the recent proposal of a member of the parliament of Canada that the name *God,* mentioned in the first sentence of the Canadian charter, be eliminated, and on the other hand, the occasional de-mand by some Americans that the United States be designated a "Christian" nation. These are the most obvious examples of the cultural debate over religion and law, but they are not the most important historically. There is little likelihood that even most secularist Canadians, in the interest of constitutional stability, would want to tamper with the opening words of the hard-won written Charter of Rights and Responsibilities. And there is lit-tle likelihood that most American Christians, even if they are in the majority, would want to make all the non-Christians in the United States mere sojourners in somebody else's house. After all, even if America were to be officially defined as a Christian nation, deciding whose Christianity makes America Christian would probably lead to the type of violence and political disrup-tion Europe saw in the sixteenth and seventeenth centuries in the wars between Catholics and Protestants, let alone to the way Jews and Muslims had been treated for a much longer period of time in Christian Europe. Surely, most Christians would want to avoid that happening again. So the most important cases are not where religion itself is the immediate subject of the debate but rather, where religion underlies the debate, and where one's re-ligious stance is the basic determining factor in moral decisions of great consequence in the lives of many citizens. A belief in the essential need for a god behind the law, or a denial of it, makes a real difference in cases that are or are likely to be landmark cases, having an effect on the development of the whole legal system thereafter and therefore a great effect on many lives in the future.

Grotius, the Stoics, and Plato on Natural Law

Although there are some ancient precedents, the notion that law can be totally secular—without a founding god—is usually taken to be a distinct feature of modernity.[10] Many locate its beginnings in a famous statement by Hugo Grotius, the early seventeenth-century Dutch Calvinist jurist, regarded as the founder of modern international law. In the "Preliminary Discourse" of his great work on international law, *De juri belli ac pacis,* Grotius writes: "And indeed, all we have now said would take place, though we should even grant [*etiamsi daremus*], what without the greatest Wickedness cannot be granted, that there is no God [*non esse Deum*], or that he takes no Care of human Affairs [*non curari ab eo negotia humana*]."[11] Shortly thereafter he continues:

> And even the Law of Nature itself [*naturale jus*], whether it be that which consists in the Maintenance of Society, or that which in a looser sense is so called, though it flows from the internal Principles of Man, may notwithstanding be justly ascribed to God [*Deo tamen adscribi merito potest*], because it was his Pleasure that these principles should be in us. And in this Sense *Chrysippus* and the *Stoicks* said, that the Original of Right is to be derived from no other than *Jupiter h*imself; from which Word *Jupiter* it is probable the *Latins g*ave it the name *Jus*.[12]

This statement of Grotius can be interpreted in one of three ways. We shall examine the two more obvious ways now, and the third, less obvious way later.

First, the most common interpretation is that given both by religious opponents of natural law and by natural law opponents of religion. For them, Grotius is saying quite clearly that there is a body of law adequate for the basic normative needs of any human society. This body of law is independent of any divine command, being fully accessible to human reason. So, "even if" (*etiamsi,* to recall Grotius's hypothesis) it is *also* a matter of divine command in biblical revelation, that is essentially superfluous to the intelligibility and practice of this law itself.

As for Grotius's disclaimer of any atheism on his own part, that could be taken as a simple concession to the political power of popular piety, which even a philosopher dare not explicitly antagonize.[13] Or, we might say more cautiously that even if Grotius the Protestant believer needs God, Grotius the legal theorist does not. Thus the God Grotius invokes is much like the God of the English deists some two centuries later, that is, a God who creates a world that is self-sufficient thereafter and who, therefore, steps out of the world picture permanently. But doesn't Grotius's God—at least along the lines of this interpretation—turn out to be a premise that the coherent explanation of the phenomenon of law does not require? Consequently, isn't this God dispensable from within the legal order by Ockham's Razor in much the same way Kant eliminated God as first cause from within the natural order?[14]

Second, this secularist interpretation would be a lot more plausible were it not for Grotius's invocation of Chrysippus and the Stoics. The Stoics clearly did not eliminate God from their thinking about anything, least of all from their thinking about law. And a good scholarly case can be made that the origins of Stoic teaching go back to Plato.[15] Thus, as the Talmud puts it rhetorically, "When we have the words of the master and the words of the disciple, to whom do we listen?"[16] Let us look then to Plato on the question of God and law for our interpretation of Grotius's suggestive statement. In so doing, we might very well discover that it is only the God of the Bible and not "the God of

the philosophers" (Pascal's famous distinction), who is dispensable for Grotius's natural law theory, or at least, for the type of
natural law theory he seems to be connecting himself to.

Plato raises this question in one of his earliest dialogues, the
Euthyphro, this way: "Is the holy [*to hosion*] loved by the gods
because it is holy [*hoti hosion*], or is it holy because it is loved
by the gods?"[17] Then Plato has Socrates get his interlocutor, the
pious Euthyphro, to agree that the holy is "a part of the just."[18]
What emerges from this is that, for Plato, the gods are not absolute, but their authority comes from their participation in
an ultimate order, which is here called "the just" [*to dikaion*].
This order is what justifies the religious claims of the gods on
humans the same way it justifies the moral claims of humans
on other humans. Developing this notion in the *Republic,* Plato
designates "the Good" as the summit of this order of eternal,
intelligible forms.[19] They are "ideas," not in the modern sense of
thoughts that are produced by human minds, but in the ancient
sense of being realities which are capable of being thought by
human minds in acts of truly intelligent discovery.

However, what is of vital importance to remember is that this
higher order is itself divine. It is divine because it is immortal.
Hence, as Antigone reminded the tyrant Creon, though he can
kill human beings, he cannot kill these divine principles. They
will still be there long after he is dead.[20] They are not subject
to the control of kings, philosophical or otherwise. That is why
natural law is much more than what is postulated by human
reason, which could just as easily take law away as give it. Human reason per se is the finite capacity of mortal beings. Human
reason intends this divine order; this order does not presuppose
human reason. It is discovered, not invented; it alone is autonomous; it is certainly more than procedure.[21] Being immortal, it
is ultimate, hence it makes claims on humans by virtue of its
irresistible attraction to all intelligences, human or godly. The
truly rational human being, one whose desire is what Plato
called philosophical eros, is one who aspires to be like the gods,

who themselves participate in divinity eternally.[22] Philosophy, including philosophical lawgiving, is the attempt to transcend our earthly, human mortality. Anything less than that cannot truly command rational human beings, or any rational being for that matter.

Along these lines, Cicero, himself a Stoic philosopher of sorts, writes:

> Therefore, since there is nothing better than reason, and since it exists both in man and God, the first common possession of man and God is reason [*prima homini cum deo rationis societas*]. But those who have reason in common must also have right reason [*recta ratio*] in common. And since right reason is Law [*sit lex*], we must believe that men have Law in common with gods. . . . Hence we must now conceive of this whole universe as one commonwealth [*una civitas communis*] of which both gods and men are members.[23]

This divine principle, unlike the God of the Bible, does not itself make the laws. But just laws, even though made by human lawgivers, must find their ultimate justification in this living principle, which Aristotle, Plato's star student, saw as the supreme activity of intelligence contemplating its own intelligibility. And Aristotle calls this reality both "the divine" (*to theion*) and "the God" (*ho theos*).[24] Nevertheless, for Aristotle, the connection between nature and human law is much more tenuous than it is with Plato. That is why the Stoic notion of law, which so greatly influenced natural law thinking in both Roman law and Catholic theology, is much more beholden to Plato than it is to Aristotle. In fact, Aristotle himself was rather ambivalent about what he called "natural justice" (*to dikaion physikon*).[25] Nevertheless, common to Plato, Aristotle, and the Stoics, "nature" (*physis*) is divine, not as the sum of all entities but rather, as the intelligible order of the universe by which all entities are governed. In the case of the human world, this is the order by which it is to be governed by those intelligent enough to be able to access it and translate it into man-made laws. Indeed, by so doing, these human lawgivers partake of divinity. Thus lawgiving is very much an act of *imitatio dei*.[26]

Since human rationality and human sociality are two sides of the same coin, this access to the cosmic order is of immediate political significance. Only a society whose law is based on nature is worthy of the moral allegiance of any rational person. Since this natural order is divine, it is different in kind from anything made by human beings by their own authority.[27] However, since this order is accessible to some human beings, these "natural lawgivers" become god-like by virtue of this very special ability. Those who are godly mediate between the immortal divine realm and the mortal human realm. Plato expresses this political need as follows:

> Cronos was aware of the fact that no human being [*anthrōpeia*] . . . is capable of having autocratic power in all human matters [*ta anthrōpina*] without becoming filled with pride [*hybrios*] and injustice [*adikias*]. So, considering this, he then appointed as kings and rulers for our cities, not men, but a breed more divine [*theioterou*]. . . . And even today this tale has a truth to tell, namely, that whenever a polity has a mortal and not a god [*theos*] for a ruler, there the people have no respite from evils and hardships. But we ought to imitate the life of the age of Cronos as it has been told and order our houses and our cities in obedience to what is immortal [*athanasias*] within us, reason's distribution [*tou nou dianomen*] being named "law" [*nomon*].[28]

One might add that something like this kind of vision reappears (minus the metaphysics, of course) when Ronald Dworkin, the most prominent Anglo-American legal theorist today, becomes almost rhapsodic when talking about the role of judges in higher courts as "princes."[29] After all, if there are "princes," doesn't that imply there is a "king"?

The Problems with Platonic-Stoic Natural Law

The usual way of looking at natural law theory is to see it coming out of this Platonic-Stoic tradition through Roman law into medieval Catholic moral theology, which had by the time of Thomas Aquinas received a thorough Aristotelian reworking.[30] In this view, natural law theory was adopted intact into the theories of Catholic theologians when they were functioning as political-legal philosophers. Those partial to this historical trajectory of natural law are not that far from the first interpretation of Grotius we examined above, which sees the mention of God, that is the God of the Bible seriously read by Calvinists like Grotius, as being a sort of concession to the belief that this God stands behind all creation, including the natural order.[31]

Nevertheless, there is a theological problem with this view of natural law, one that could be sensed by anyone who, like Pascal, understands that the God of Abraham, Isaac, and Jacob—that is the God of the Jews and the Christians—is not the same as the god of the Greek philosophers. It was a problem most acutely sensed by the Protestant Reformers in their revolt against the type of scholastic theology that seemed to so easily elide the great divide between the god of the philosophers and the God of the Bible. But whereas the god of the philosophers could make the God of the Bible part of a larger divine realm, the God of the Bible who tolerates "no other gods besides Me" (Exod. 20:3) could not be so tolerant.

In this view, which Grotius merely (and rather crudely) appropriated, the presence of the creator God of the Bible is not required for the natural order (including the human political order) to be intelligible for us. Accordingly, this biblical God seems to be confined to the realm of dogmatic theology. In this natural law theory, there seems to be room only for the god of Plato. The God of the Bible, who calls himself "the first" (*ri'shon*) and "the last" (*aharon*—Isa. 44:6), could hardly be confused with the god of Plato. Plato's god is a person like the God of the Bible, but hardly the person who is absolute, let alone the One who transcends the world as its creator *ex nihilo*—out of nothing— and *per nihilum*—by means of nothing. Plato's god requires the forms above and chaos beneath him in order to engender—that is, "in-form"—the cosmos.[32] The forms above this god are clearly transpersonal, engaging in no transitive action, let alone trans- actional relationships with anyone beneath them.

The idea of a supreme will, answerable to no form above and needing no matter below, would have been the height of absur- dity for Plato. So there is a problem with the Jews and Chris- tians in our society who affirm natural law. How is it really con- sistent with their own theology of creation, let alone with the centrality of historical revelation in both of these monotheistic traditions? That is the theological problem, which has led many Protestant Christians and even many more traditional Jews to see natural law theory as a dangerous rival to the law of the God of Abraham, Isaac, and Jacob. And even many Catholic theo- logians today acknowledge that natural law theory, which has been an integral constituent of their moral theology, requires more profound theological grounding to be religiously valid. The only god the natural law theory beholden to Plato and the Stoics seems to require is not the God Jews and Christians live and die for. For those who like this sort of dichotomy, natural law seems to be on the Athenian side of an unbridgeable chasm between Athens (the city of the philosophers) and Jerusalem (the city of the biblical prophets). "What indeed has Athens to do with Jerusalem?!" as the early Christian theologian Tertul- lian put it.[33]

The theological problem leads right into the political prob- lem. Here the problem with this theology is that it assumes that the natural law, in which one can see a secular polity grounded, is a maximalist law. That is, it assumes that it is sufficient to govern everything that transpires within the polity. This type of maximalism poses a political problem because it seems to require for its interpretation and application the type of exceptional human minds who can see the higher truths unavailable to the lesser minds of ordinary citizens. It is the problem of much natural law theory presented by theologians. Quite often, they argue for a natural law in principle knowable by all, but in fact knowable only through those to whom revelation has been entrusted. This leads to a kind of elitism of which most citizens of democracies are so rightly suspicious. This elitism is not only most obvious in such seemingly obsolete notions as the "divine right of kings," but also in the exalted, almost mystical, role assigned to judges in constitutional democracies.[34] Most citizens of a democracy are suspicious of this kind of all-inclusive political thinking because the hallmark of a modern constitutional democracy seems to be minimalism.

When it comes to more elevated existential needs than those of political stability and order, most of us do not look to secular society for their fulfillment. Instead, most of us look to communities whose vision is far more cosmic than that of civil society, where that which orders life is much greater than what we can mundanely discover. We look to communities whose story transmits a unique revelation for those who have accepted it. The secular order is contained and therefore protected best when the line between sacred and "profane" space is clear. The original meaning of the Latin *profanus* is "what is before the entrance to the temple," that is, what has been carved out of the holy. The "secular" comes from the *saeculum,* that which is ephemeral in relation to an unending realm beyond it. The very containment of the political order of civil society, and the very fact that its principles are taken to be immediately intelligible to any normal human being, is most forcefully argued when our more maximal existential needs are fulfilled elsewhere. The fulfillment of these needs requires the direct word of God.

The secular realm can only deal with whatever truth we can discover *from* our ordinary or usual or predictable experience of the world. We call the intelligible object of that mundane experience "nature." Revelation, conversely, is what is given *to* us from beyond the world. As such, it is not ordinary, not usual, and not predictable. We call the supermundane object of that experience "logos." It speaks to us before we can speak or reason about it. Nevertheless, what both kinds of experience have in common is that we can reason about both of them—that is, as long as our reasoning about both kinds of experience does not presume to deduce the reality of the object of either experience from its own operations.³⁵ In fact, we need to speak about both kinds of experience since we need to apply them to our lives in the world. Even revelation, though not being *of* the world is still *in* it, and speech is the very hallmark of human being in the world. "The Torah speaks according to human language [*ke-lashon benei adam*]."³⁶ Indeed, how could the Torah speak in any other language and still be understood by the humans to whom it is given? That being the case, the epistemological divide is not, as many still think, between "reason and revelation" but rather, between *nature* and *revelation*. In relation to nature, we bring *logos* to it: we *bespeak* it. In relation to revelation, we unpack the *logos* that has already been spoken to us. Thus in relation to nature, our intention of its transcendent object is only done to negate any creative pretensions of human reason claiming to be more than a heuristic tool. But in relation to revelation, our intention of it as a transcendent source is an act of positive affirmation.

The very limit on human making—including human social construction, so dear to the partisans of democracy—is best maintained when the majority of the citizens of a democracy look to *logos* rather than to nature for the fulfillment of what can be shown to be the irrepressible need to be related to the transcendent. Since the recognition of this need, let alone its fulfillment, is a sign of the true value of human nature, it stands to reason that we first recognize that value, that dignity, in the way we order the more mundane sphere of civil society, which deals with the needs of the body, physical and political. We cannot attend to the needs of the soul by short-circuiting the needs of the body. However, when that soulful or "spiritual" need becomes distorted into salvific visions of civil society itself, the democratic commonality of civil society is the first victim of this spiritual distortion, usually through elitist-type programs, frequently theorized by politicians who think themselves to be philosophers, or even by philosophers whose claim to the title has wider agreement.

And finally, Platonic-Stoic natural law theory has a problem with its political paradigm. This comes out most acutely when we notice how all of its versions in one form or another involve the notion of human and social perfectibility. That moral vision needs to be undergirded by a teleological vision of human history, even if it does not need a teleological vision of the cosmos as a whole, a vision that has been banished from natural science beginning with Galileo.[37]

In the Platonic version, human reason—properly and fully exercised by quasi-divine humans in the right society—by looking to divine nature or natural divinity, can lead that society to the end of all ends of all cosmic striving. In the Stoic version, which comes in the wake of the attempt of Alexander the Great and his Hellenistic (as distinct from what in Plato's time would have only been "Hellenic," that is, ethnically Greek) successors to make the whole world speak Greek, we see that teleological vision extended to the larger domain of human history.[38] And in fact, despite key differences, this Hellenistic vision (in which Stoicism participated) of the unity of civilization contributed to a climate of eschatological expectation in late antiquity that made many pagans find Jewish and Christian messianic visions so attractive. Nevertheless, this marriage of Greek teleology and Hebraic eschatology always seemed to forget that political and cultural imperialism inevitably becomes the vehicle for the hu-

man achievement of the end of human history. In biblical eschatology, however, the end time is apocalyptic: it will be accomplished by divine intervention in human history, not by any
human forcing of the end of history.[39]

Historical teleology or secular eschatology, the type of speculation most impressively presented by Hegel, has been largely
abandoned due to the findings of cultural anthropology, which
have shown how the notion of a progressive trajectory in human
history is the construction of the cultural imperialism of the
"Eurocentrism" of the West. In fact, this modern cultural imperialism bears strong resemblance to the cultural imperialism of
the Alexandrian-Hellenistic Age, in its attempt to get the whole
world to speak and think Greek, and the more blatantly political
imperialism of the Roman Empire, in its attempt to govern the
whole world. What we seem to have is a variety of communal
and cultural histories, with no way to judge whether any one of
them is in the true vanguard of historical progress culminating
in the end of history.

Yet to leave matters at this point is to leave us in the moral
dead end of relativism, where we have nothing more than the
very ephemeral negotiation of competing and conflicting self-
interest of individuals and groups. In common with the Platonic-Stoic natural law theory, we cannot settle for any natural law
without a god behind it, because the immortality of a god is the
only power that can possibly contain the human violence that
would destroy our lives, both separately and together. And only
a god is superior enough in power and in wisdom to all humans
for any human to listen to its commands without being able to
say: who are you to tell me what to do?[40] It is our human propen-
sity for violence (in many forms) that propels us to seek a modus
vivendi worthy of the allegiance of a plurality of persons from a
plurality of historical cultures. So we need to find another ontological basis for a more cogent natural law, with a different
epistemology to make it more persuasive for our political needs
here and now.

Covenantal Theology

In the Platonic-Stoic version of natural law, the role of reason is maximal. In the covenantal theology of the Bible, and the traditions of Judaism and Christianity built upon it, the role of reason is minimal. However, contrary to the claims of some orthodox believers, whether Jewish or Christian (or Islamic in the larger context of monotheism), the minimal role of human reason in this theology is not reduced to the point of nonexistence. And that small, but necessary, role for human reason is not just a posteriori, that is, it is not only to interpret revelation exegetically in the form of commentary. It also has an a priori role, that is, it can operate independently of revelation, prior to it, though ultimately for revelation rather than against it. Indeed, with more modest demands being made upon it, human reason actually functions much better than when it usurps revelation's role in human life. A sound talmudic principle is: "when one grabs the maximum, one loses everything; when one grabs the minimum, one thereby gets something."[41]

At this point, let us return to Grotius's statement about the possibility of law "even if we say there is no God." We have seen how Grotius' invocation of the Stoics could lead us to believe that he is substituting the god of Plato for the God of the Bible, which means placing God under the rule of the law's ultimate paradigm. Looking at that line of thought, we have seen its intellectual splendor, but we have also seen the problems it raises for us here and now: theologically, philosophically, and politically. Nevertheless, we should also remember that Grotius quotes the Bible to illustrate his points about the foundations of law. And considering the fact that he was a Calvinist Christian, the burden of proof is on those who would judge him to be a crypto-atheist, and even on those who would see his invocation of the Stoics as being more significant theologically than his invocation of the God of the Bible. Perhaps it is best to see Grotius's statement in the light of the biblical theology that was so dominant in the

Netherlands (and elsewhere) both before, during, and long after Grotius's time. In so doing, we might discover a biblically authorized natural law, one that is consistent with biblical theology, but one whose precepts and whose theory need not be derived by the exegesis of specific biblical passages, especially not from explicit biblical precepts, even though these precepts might well be presupposed by biblical teaching.[42]

If a natural law theory without some kind of god soon becomes incoherent, then Grotius's statement might well be saying: even without the invocation of a certain mode of God's action, we can still have natural law. We have seen how that interpretation works in the Platonic sense of a divine realm above the function of the individual gods. Regarding biblical theology, we of course cannot posit a divine realm above the individual gods, since there is only one God. It makes no sense to posit a separate divine realm from the person of God when there is only one member of such a realm. Only a plurality of members of a class prevents any one of them from becoming identical with the class itself.

The way to interpret Grotius's statement that preserves an idea of natural law and is faithful to the God of the Bible worshiped by Jews and Christians is to look to the ways the Bible names God. Despite the essential difference between biblical monotheism and Platonic polytheism, there is nevertheless more than one name for God in the Bible. That means that the one God manifests himself in more than one way. The two most frequently used names of God in the Bible are *elohim,* usually translated as "God" (*theos* in Greek; *deus* in Latin), and the ineffable tetragrammaton YHWH, for which "the name of the Lord" is always substituted (*adonai* in Hebrew; *kyrios* in Greek; *dominus* in Latin). A good case can be made that frequently enough "God" (*elohim*) is used to designate God as creator of the world and who sustains the world by engendering a permanent order within it.[43]

Unlike the Platonic idea of nature, this order of creation does not transcend what it orders; hence its presence does not signify the eternity of the world. It simply means that as long as the world exists, its order, its essential structure, will be coeval with it. Nevertheless, this order does transcend all the powers within the world. The whole is greater than any one of its parts, but not to all of them in concert. All relations, then, are external to the parts, but internal to the cosmos. The cosmos does not contain its parts; it exists among them, not round about them or over them. The internality of the cosmos is its inherent order, its *mishpat* in biblical terms, which is "justice" in the widest possible sense.[44] The tetragrammaton, on the other hand, designates the God who has elected Israel and is continually involved with Israel in a special covenantal relationship. "God" is the master of created nature; "the Lord" is, in addition to God's natural role, the master of historical revelation and historical redemption. "God" names the more universal but less intense acts of God; "the Lord" names the more intense but less universal (at least here and now) acts of God. Perhaps we might surmise that Grotius is reiterating a theological tradition that says that some of God's law can be known without a direct revelation from God? In other words, we could say that "no God" (*non esse Deum*) here means "no revealed God."

Let us see how the particular name of God we invoke gives ontological foundation to the natural law we see ourselves duty bound to obey. This requires seeing the political context of the law.

The key political term in the Bible is *berit,* usually translated "covenant." It denotes the essential context of all worldly relationships. We tend to confuse a "covenant" with a "contract" and so use the words interchangeably. That is unfortunate, since a covenant is much more than a contract. Indeed, as we shall see later, a contract is actually a diminished covenant, and one whose integrity gets lost when the covenantal connection is severed. Accordingly, whereas the idea of contract can be derived from the idea of covenant, a covenant cannot be seen as merely a glorified contract without distorting the idea of both relationships.[45] A covenant is a relationship between two persons initiated and renewed in promises of fidelity made by each one to the other.

The first covenant God makes with creation after human violence almost destroys mankind and the earthly order along with them at the time of the flood. In this covenant, God promises the perpetuity of the natural order to Noah and his descendents. "As long as there is seedtime and harvest, the cold and the hot, summer and winter, the days of the earth shall not cease " (Gen. 8:22). And directly following this, the minimal task of humans in the world are ordered. These tasks are to procreate, and thus carve out of the larger wilderness a world fit for continued human dwelling, and to control violence so that this human dwelling not be destroyed as it nearly was when Cain murdered his brother Abel and when nature was perverted at the time of the flood. The reason for both of these primary tasks seems to be the same, being expressed as follows: "Whosoever sheds the blood of a human, by humans his own blood shall be shed, because in the image of God God made humans" (Gen. 9:6).

By the term the "image of God," the Bible seems to be saying that it is human nature to be related to God, that this unique relationship in creation is always a possibility for humans and a reality for God. Humans, in their full communal nature, are the objects of unique divine concern. Accordingly, they are to be the objects of unique concern for each other. Indeed, in any earthly transaction, both the subject and the object are functioning as the image of God: the subject stands as a reflection of man's concern for God, and the object stands as a reflection of God's concern for man. Indeed, in the natural world—that is, the world not based on historical revelation—the claims of the creator God on his creatures are totally mediated by the justifiable claims one human being makes upon another. These claims are direct and evident to all. They do not require prophetic revelation, either through one prophet to his community or to a whole community as occurred at the covenant at Sinai.

The fact that God promises to let created nature in general endure establishes enough of an atmosphere for human nature to endure specifically. The duration of nature is a tangible result of God's faithfulness (*emunah*). Truth (*emet*), then, is the internal coherence of the natural order, a sign that it is endurable because of God's faithfulness to it. That is why our words can coherently correspond to it. It holds together so that we can say something consistent about it.[46] Since human nature is the epitome of the natural order created by God, our faithful response to God's faithfulness to creation and its inseparable order is demonstrated in how faithful we are to the legitimate needs of our fellow human beings, both individual and communal. One could say that human nature is the sum of essential human needs, that is, those needs that a satisfactory life for any human being require. In a biblical sense, that is what could well be called "natural law." It is where our fidelity to the world and God's fidelity to the world coincide. It is what the Bible calls "the way of all the earth" [*derekh kol ha'arets*], and what the ancient rabbis called *derekh erets*, which might be translated "the proper way to conduct oneself within the world."[47] Indeed, since the Bible describes this *derekh erets*, but does not prescribe it, presupposing it as it were, one could also infer that it is something learned from the world. It is not derived from the voice of God directly speaking to us in revelation; instead, it is the echo of the voice of God that reverberates from our experience with our fellow humans in our joint task to make the world a dwelling and not a cemetery. God speaks *through* their just claims upon one another and *through* their just responses to one another.[48] As such, God is ultimately both the subject and the object of the law governing all these rights and correlative duties.

The main motif of biblical moral teaching is covenantal faithfulness. It is considered to be in the nature of human beings to make various covenants with each other, and all of these covenants look to the covenant at the time of Noah as their basic form. Furthermore, the covenantal character of biblical morality indicates a more dynamic quality to a society that looks to it as its political model than one finds in a society that looks to Platonic-Stoic natural law ethics as its political model. The reason for this difference is that in Platonic-Stoic ethics—what Leo Strauss liked to call "classical natural right"—natural law is taken to be the maximum general structure of all human relationships.[49] As such, it functions like an Aristotelian genus, *within which* all more specific human relationships are subsets.

In more Platonic conceptuality, one can see the events of human histories as either being instantiations of the known form of justice or denials of it. One has to know the whole before knowing the parts therein.[50] But in biblical morality, whose basic norms are not derived from but presupposed by biblical revelation, these basic norms do not function as a genus with everything that follows being its subordinate specification. There is always the possibility of new relationships that could not be deduced from the basic norms of the old law. The most that is asked of the formulation of these new relationships is that they not contradict the law already in place, and that they be consistent with what are seen to be the overall purposes of the Torah itself.

The contracts made between human beings are an example of the type of covenants that build upon the primary covenants without being directly derived from them. In much the same way, the covenant of Sinai built upon the Noahide covenant without being reduced to it. All that is required is that what is new not directly contradict the specifics of what has already been received.[51] Furthermore, the messianic promise of "a new heaven and a new earth" will nonetheless not eliminate the Israel of the original covenant at Sinai, who will still "stand before Me" (Isa. 66:22).[52] The promise that God's store of faithfulness has not yet been exhausted can provide a powerful paradigm for the faithful potential of human beings in their relationships among themselves.

This feature of biblical morality has been a very important source for the main mode of political arrangement in our Western liberal democracies: the social contract. The question is: can the social contract, or any contract, be totally severed from its covenantal roots? If it can be so severed, then we can locate the point in history when the notion of a totally secular law really took hold. But if it cannot be so severed, then we are either forced back to these covenantal roots or we wind up with an insufficient idea of social contract altogether.

Social Contract

As noted earlier, Hugo Grotius is considered to be the founder of modern natural right theory as well as the founder of modern international law. Indeed, these two roles can be closely correlated. The point of correlation is the centrality of contract in both spheres. International law, especially the law of the seas, was something vital to the interests of Grotius's nation, the Netherlands, a small but highly ambitious trading nation at the time. The political security required for sustained and successful international trade can only be based on contract, since the parties to international trade have heretofore been separated by nature or history or both. They must therefore create their relationship de novo by mutual agreement. The Calvinism of Grotius's Netherlands prepared him and the whole society he served, in an official as well as a theoretical capacity, for this new challenge because of its immense preoccupation with the biblical idea of covenant. A contract is derivative of covenant: both have a temporal beginning, a *terminus a quo*; unlike a covenant, though, a contract can also have a temporal end, a *terminus ad quem*.

The English Puritans of the seventeenth century closely followed the biblically based political theology of their Calvinist brethren in the Netherlands, especially the emphasis on covenant. So we see this well expressed by the Puritan divine William Perkins, who in 1624 wrote: "We are by nature covenant creatures, bound together by covenants innumerable and together bound by our covenant to our God. Such is our human condition. Such is this earthly life. Such is God's good creation. Blest be the ties that bind us."[53]

Of course, Plato's natural law theory also recognized contracts. Certainly, it is rationally evident that by definition contracts are to be kept, that persons are to do what they say they will do. It is the practical issue of truthfulness, which Plato would see as the translation of the theoretical value of truth into human action. Nevertheless, it is also clear from the teaching of Plato and his heirs that a society founded on a contract, that is, an interpersonal agreement, is inferior to a society founded on the eternal order of nature.[54] For this reason, then, the development of contract theory did not find a place in classical natural law theory. Looking to an eternal order would make one highly suspicious of any innovations. Innovations such as contracts are only a necessity at times; they are not a permanent desideratum. Platonic-type natural law theory is much more concerned with status than with contract. Thus Plato's definition of justice as "what is owed to one [*ta opheilomena hekasto*] is to be given to him."[55] That became a cornerstone of the *Corpus Juris Civilis*, namely, "to give each what is his own" (*suum cuique tribuere*).[56]

The emphasis on contracts, both between private parties and between individual nations, was quite prominent in the Netherlands, and in its commercial and political rival, England. Both nations being Protestant polities and both having a renewed interest in distinctly biblical theology no doubt gave a theological impetus for this otherwise mundane preoccupation. Following this interest in the very phenomenon of contract, it is understandable how the idea of contract became prominent in the great debates that took place in both countries about the foundations of polity itself. Could the very foundation of a society, its political and legal legitimacy, be seen as a contract between the individual members of the society and their state? Could the res publica themselves be seen as contractual in essence? Could the state be founded in a *social contract*? And for some who were eager to explore that theoretical route, it seemed that there could indeed be a basis for society found neither in nature or revelation, that is, neither in the god of Plato nor in the God of the Bible. If so, could we at long last interpret—or reinterpret—Grotius's "even if we say there is no God" in the most radical way possible, namely, "even were we to say there is no God at all," or "there is no God with whom or to whom humans can be related at all"? These questions bring us straight to the portals of Thomas Hobbes.

The key difference between Hobbes's natural law theory on the one hand, and Platonic natural law theory and the covenantal theology of the Bible on the other hand, is whether the location of our earthly nature is a dwelling we can care for or an inferno we can only protect ourselves from. That inferno is what Hobbes saw as natural right, namely, "the liberty each man hath, to use his own power, as he will himself, for the preservation of his own nature; that is to say, of his own life."[57] That natural liberty is an entirely individual matter as, for instance, when a thief says, "It is my nature to take whatever I want whenever I want it." At this elementary level, there is no trust whatsoever between persons, who are competing for what are always scarce resources, other than the most ephemeral utility, what Plato saw as being like the temporary agreements of a band of thieves.[58] It is everyone for himself. There is a total absence of the kind of sustained and sustainable trust a genuine human community presupposes.[59] It is "everybody warring against everybody else" (*bellum omnium contra omnes*).[60]

Hobbes is acutely aware that no society can be based on this type of terrifying anarchy. But how can we get people to keep their word to others, that is, to engage in the type of contract-making that is so necessary for any society, and especially for a commercially ambitious society, to endure? The answer is that at this level persons are so terrified of the loss of their lives and property at the hands of others that they are willing to sacrifice all their natural liberty to a superhuman creature who will protect them all for the price of their obedience. Whatever liberty citizens of the state have left after this irrevocable bargain is liberty that is too trivial for the state to bother with, hence it is what the state in effect gives back to its citizens as a sort of revocable entitlement.[61]

Hobbes recognized that the ordinary business of society, especially in a society where the greater equality among the rising commercial class was fast replacing the greater inequality of the old feudal order with its more fixed status levels, was becoming more and more structured by more flexible contractual arrangements. The main questions he had to answer was: Why should people be faithful to their contacts? Why should people keep the promises that initiate these contractual relationships?

Hobbes's answer about the power of the state to enforce contracts, first and foremost the social contract between the state and its citizens, is based on the absolute priority of the power of the state. Like the myth of Gyges' Ring in Plato's *Republic,* Hobbes assumes that human beings, left to their own devices—which would be the case if they were invisible to public scrutiny— would not be capable of the self-sacrifice required for anyone to keep his or her word to another person.[62] Everyone would be everyone else's enemy or at best, everyone else's "fair-weather friend," which might be worse, inasmuch as one can be more certain of an enemy than a supposed friend.

We might not like this very grim view of human nature, but it does have a chilling correspondence with the way many people look at the juncture between the private and the public realms. Moreover, it coherently correlates the three main elements of a contract: (1) the promise that initiates it, (2) the possible actions and reactions it governs, and (3) the threat of penalty for violating it. The logical order that emerges from Hobbes's constitution of contract is: against the background of penalties for possible violations, persons feel secure enough to make contractual promises to one another, and to set out the actions and reactions the contract is to govern. Thus the threat of a penalty is not a subsequent aspect of a promise but rather, it makes the very promise possible. The contract does not entail a threat; it presupposes a threat already in place. As such, it would seem that the power of the state is already present in order for citizens to contract themselves to it. It is not something they themselves make up at will and can thus tear down at will.

Considering how basically self-serving human beings are, no promise would be possible if the matter were left to simple trust *ab initio*. Fear of harmful consequences, then, is the greatest manifestation of that self-interest. As Hobbes puts it, "There must be some coercive power, to compel men equally to the performance of their covenants, by the terror of some punishment, greater than the benefit they expect by the breach of their covenant."[63] And at this point, Hobbes reveals the "divine" character of this "coercive power." It is "that great Leviathan, or rather, to speak more reverently, of that *mortal* god, to which we owe under the *immortal God,* our peace and defense."[64] Of course, the irony of asserting a "mortal god" is that the very term is an oxymoron. Whether in Jerusalem or in Athens, a "god" by definition is immortal.

Following this line of thought, though, one could well ask whether or not the power of this "mortal god" is consistent with the power of the immortal God who, for Hobbes's readers is, no doubt, the covenanting God of the Bible. After all, isn't Hobbes's notion of contract quite similar to biblical notions of covenant? Doesn't the Bible threaten God's punishment if the covenant between God and his people is broken? The people are told, "You shall keep the words of this covenant and do them in order that you might succeed" (Deut. 29:8), and anyone who violates it is threatened with "all the curses of the covenant written in this book of the Torah" (29:20). And as the Talmud tells it in a theologically charged vision, God held Mount Sinai over Israel's head and told them, in effect, "Accept the Torah or else."[65]

Furthermore, if divine punishment lies at the heart of the biblical covenant, then isn't the state acting in place of God? In fact, Hobbes points out that "before the time of civil society . . . there is nothing can strengthen a covenant of peace agreed on, against the temptations of avarice, lust, or other strong desire, but the fear of that invisible power, which they every one worship as God; and fear as a revenger of their perfidy."[66] How does that differ from the Noahide covenant established after the destruction of the Flood? Doesn't God first say, "Surely your life-blood will I demand from every beast and from the hand of humans" (Gen. 9:5), followed by "whosoever sheds human blood, by humans shall his blood be shed, for in the image of God He made humans" (9:6)? In other words, human justice is mandated to act, partially to be sure, on behalf of divine justice. Accordingly, if the relationship with the immortal God is totally mediated by the relationship with the king as "that mortal god," then how does it differ from it? Using the logic of Ockham's Razor, isn't the assumption of a heavenly God above an earthly god, but totally subject to this earthly god's judgments, isn't that assumption ultimately superfluous? Or following the logic of Feuerbach, who argued that "God" is merely a projection of humans on to the cosmos, doesn't any differentiation between the God of the Bible and the god of Hobbes turn out to be a semantic distinction without an ontological difference?[67]

Contract as Promise

Despite some important philosophical differences between Hobbes's theory of contract and that of adherents to the "divine right of kings," both theories assume that all interhuman agreements, whether they be between individual humans among themselves or between all the citizens and the state, are basically enforceable because of the fear of punishment for noncompliance. The adherents of both theories were in favor of the royal status quo, a status that was being challenged in seventeenth-century England, and which was overturned in 1649 with the regicide of Charles I by the Puritan Oliver Cromwell and his followers. Both Hobbes and the "theological royalists" were opposed to the Puritan challenge to that status quo, which invoked biblical ideas of covenant as an alternative to the seemingly unfettered exercise of royal authority. The tragedy was, however, that the Puritans did not work out a biblically based political theory that could successfully counter the theory of the divine right of kings, much less the more philosophically astute theory of Hobbes. That is why their own regime in New England quickly became as autocratic as the Stuart regime from which they fled.[68] They too seemed to be primarily interested in their own power to assign social roles rather than relying more on the capacity of persons to contract their own social roles based on trust among themselves.

One could say that this Puritan failure on both the theoretical and practical levels was due to their own theology being much more concerned with divine punishment as a consequence of breach of the covenant than with the divine faithfulness that is the antecedent, the ground of the covenant itself. Yet when it comes to punishment, it seems that the punishment of the state is more immediately experienced than the punishment of God. At this point, one is reminded of Stalin's famous quip about how many divisions the pope has. Fear of punishment as the basis of a political order makes the kingdom of God look rather puny compared to the power of the earthly kings. As the Bible puts it, "Not by power [be-hayil] and not by might [be-koah], but by my spirit [be-ruhi], saith the Lord of Hosts" (Zech. 4:6).[69] The spirit of God must be understood as operating very differently than does the police power of the state. So what is the difference?

To answer this question, we need a phenomenology of human agreement itself. This involves asking the most basic question, namely: why should I believe your commitment to me to do what you promise to do with me? In other words, why should I accept you as my contractual partner? We have already seen one answer to this question: you can believe my commitment to you in what I promise to do with you because I fear the legal consequences of breach of contract. But that does not involve trust, and most of us see trust as an essential element in our human agreements. Many of us would not enter into an agreement with a person we regarded as untrustworthy, even if we were assured that we would not suffer loss by the breach of contract this untrustworthy person would probably commit. Breach of contract provisions in the law are like a life insurance policy: we want to know it is there, but we act as if it weren't there. In other words, we make provisions in the event of death, but we act now as if we are to live forever. Death is a hidden horizon we prepare for, but it is not the purpose of our action here and now. So too is it with fear of punishment. Similarly, we want a breach of contract to be punished; but we do not want the threat of punishment to be the prime motivation for a contractual partner to keep his or her word to us.

The primacy of trust itself is brought out quite well by contemporary legal theorist Charles Fried in his book on the foundations of contract law. He writes, "So remarkable a tool is trust that in the end we pursue it for its own sake; we prefer doing things cooperatively when we might have relied on fear or interest or worked alone."[70] That is a powerful insight, one designed to turn our thinking away from making contracts simply the instruments of our selfish interests. Thus Fried implies that contracts must be seen as a specific manifestation of a deeper mode of interrelationship between persons. Could we not say it reflects an innate covenantal desire on our part? Nevertheless, Fried does not ask the obvious question: why should I trust you? All of us learn quite early in life that there are some people we can trust and others we cannot trust. What makes one person trustworthy and another person undeserving of my trust?

So why should I trust you? It would seem that my trust depends on some knowledge of your character, of the type of person experience teaches me that you have been in the past and are likely to remain in the future. Surely, I trust someone whom I either know or who is reputed to be law abiding. *He or she is*

*someone who will not change his word to me because he is com-
mitted to an unchanging word.* The promise to me, then, must be
part of that larger, more lasting, commitment. Since humans in
and of themselves are mortal and thus subject to the greatest of
all changes—death—their commitment has to be to an immortal word, one not subject to death, the change of all changes. In
biblical language: "The grass withers and the flower fades, but
the word of our God endures forever" (Isa. 40:8).[71] For biblical believers, God's faithfulness to creation and its veridical order is to
be imitated by human fidelity to it, especially by rational discovery of the authentic rights inherent in created human nature.[72]

What does that mean? It means that I now have good reason
to trust you to keep your word to me because you are personally
committed to a law or standard not of your own making. You
will not be disloyal to your word to me because you are loyal to
the word laid upon you by a power higher than yourself or any
other mortal human like yourself. That is why I can trust you
and thus desire to develop a social relationship with you and all
others like you. Because you are committed to truth in the way it
has been shown to you, I can be reasonably sure that you will not
deceive me. Minimally, a commitment to truth involves my saying what I mean and doing what I say. My commitment to truth
begins in my abhorrence of liars and hypocrites. Liars construct
the truth to suit their own whims; similarly, hypocrites affirm
the truth in speech while denying it in deed.

Does this mean, then, when the social contract is not based
on the elevation of the state to godlike status as it is for Hobbes
and those who followed him, it can only be affirmed in good
faith (in the original sense of bona fides) by those who have a
god? In other words, can an atheist be trusted? This question is
always thrown up to religious people by those who are quick to
point out that there are plenty of virtuous atheists and plenty of
religious scoundrels. A too-hasty answer to this question gets
religious people into the position of having to affirm a religious
test for citizenship in a democracy, and that is just as undemo-

cratic as those doctrinaire secularists who seem determined to outlaw religion incrementally, step-by-step. The answer to the question hinges on what one means by atheism. The classic rabbinic answer was to identify as an atheist one who followed the Hellenistic philosopher Epicurus (hence they were called in Hebrew *apiqorsim*) who, it will be recalled, did not deny the possibility that there are gods in the sense of superhuman cosmic causes—a possibility that cannot be proven to be impossible.[73] What the Epicureans denied was that even if these gods do exist somewhere, they have no interest in human affairs, let alone any interest in judging human affairs.[74] Thus the rabbis said such a person is one who denies that there is a law and that there is a judge (*leit din ve-leit dayyan*).[75] But is there any such person?

Certainly, in private there are such persons. For example, the type of princes for whom Machiavelli wrote are those persons who saw the fulfillment of their desires for power or whatever as being their primary motivation.[76] And it is a mistake, I think, for religious people to quickly conclude that such egotists or libertines have a god too in the object of their desire. Since they so identify themselves with their desires, there is not enough externality here to warrant calling the objects of these desires "gods." Because our desires themselves do not manifest themselves to us in lawlike fashion—that is, as *nomos*—it is a mistake to render our unencumbered fulfillment of them "autonomy." The gods come into the picture when persons seek public approval of their own desires. Thus the "morally debased person who says in his heart 'there is no God'" (Ps. 53:2) only says that in private.[77] In public, this same person must acknowledge some judging authority, who if not a god must function like one, so that other people will want to do business with him or her and not lock their doors every time he approaches.

In public, everyone must invoke some god or other because there everyone has to speak normatively. One cannot participate in any public activity without acknowledging the need for law. The best example of that is speech itself, which requires laws of grammar in order to be intelligible, laws which no one speaker of a language could arbitrarily make for himself or herself alone. Thus grammar is how speakers of a language require each other to speak in a way that makes sense.[78] Hence, just as a speaker desirous of promoting his or her point of view requires the prior guarantee of grammar to get that point of view across to others, so any person participating in society requires the prior guarantee of law in order to fulfill his or her personal desires. And surely, the fulfillment of these personal desires involves relations with other persons already there with us in society. (The primacy of eros as the archetype of all desire makes this point most strongly, since eros always involves another person.) But if law is to intelligently order our interpersonal desires in such a way that the common good is properly served, how could that law be the product of the desires of any of those who need to be governed by it? Thus it must come from the desire or will of someone not governed by it. Once there is an externally imposed law on our desires, here is a god of some sort or other. It would seem that we only want to obey someone generically different from and superior to ourselves. Thus, for example, once we discover our parents are generically similar to ourselves, that they are mortal like us and we like them, we have already divested them of the godlike status they had in our infancy. We now honor and respect them because of the command of the everlasting God who is different in kind both from us and from them.[79] The question, then, is not a god or no-god. The question is *whose* god.[80]

From what we have seen so far, there are really only three such gods (at least for those in the West): the God of the Bible, Platonic divinity, and Hobbes's divinized state. The question for worshipers of the God of the Bible is how they can relate to worshipers of these other two gods. Furthermore, can the worshipers of the God of the Bible show whether the worship of the Platonic divinity or the worship of Hobbes's divinized state is a better basis for a commitment to a democratic social contract than the other?

Jerusalem and Athens

One might well assume that the worshipers of the God of the Bible could not find any common ground with the worshipers of any other god. After all, isn't the Decalogue quite explicit about the insistence of the Lord God of Israel that there "be no other gods besides Me [*elohim aherim al panei*]" (Exod. 20:3)? Yet the matter is not so either-or, for when the Hebrew Bible (Old Testament) is examined carefully, one must conclude that there is no specific prohibition of the nations of the world from worshiping their own gods. In fact, there is explicit recognition of this as their right. "Let all of the nations, every one of them, walk in the name of its god, but we shall walk in the name of the Lord our God forever" (Mic. 4:5). The prohibition of idolatry and the numerous admonitions about it are all directed to Israel. It is Israel who is covenanted to the Lord God. Any deviation from that exclusive covenant toward any other god is not to be tolerated by "the Lord your God, who is a jealous God" (Exod. 20:5). The pagan gods are reviled and ridiculed only when they are attractive to Israel. "For all the goods of the peoples are mere nothings, but the Lord made the heavens" (Ps. 96:5). Nevertheless, these same heavenly bodies are considered to be the rightful objects of gentile devotion among themselves. "Lest you lift up your eyes to the heavens and you be swept away and bow down to them and serve them, which the Lord your God has assigned [*halaq*] to all the peoples under the heavens" (Deut. 4:19).[81]

There are suggestions in the Bible itself, which are further developed in post-biblical Jewish theology, that the divide between covenanted Israel and the noncovenanted nations of the world might not be so absolute on the question of God. Slowly the notion developed that the difference between Israel and the gentiles is not that Israel worships the Creator and the gentiles worship exalted creatures but rather, that Israel worships the Creator directly and the gentiles worship the Creator indirectly through the mediation of beings who are less than divine but more than human. These intermediary beings are assigned the status of angels [mal'akhim]. Thus the verse "He established the borders of the peoples according to the number of the number [le-mispar] of the children of Israel" (Deut. 32:8) is rendered in the Septuagint "according to the number of the angels [tōn angelōn] of God." This translation or paraphrase makes sense when we look at the verse that follows it directly: "for the portion [heleq] of the Lord is his people" (32:9). By making the gods of the nations the angels of the One God, it is now asserted that the ultimate intention of the worship of the gentiles is the same One God that Israel worships directly because of its covenantal portion. Furthermore, even long before the rise of Christian and Islamic monotheism, it was recognized that everyone who invokes the name "God" ultimately intends the same God. So the last of the canonical Hebrew prophets, Malachi, states: "From the rising to the setting of the sun My name is great among the nations, and in every place incense and pure offerings are brought for My name; for great is My name among the nations, so says the Lord [YHWH] of the heavenly host" (Mal. 1:11).

From all this it follows why a worshiper of the God of the Bible has good reason to trust a philosophical advocate of classical natural law teaching. Trust is possible here because such a person is already faithful to a normative order not of his or her own making, even if that fidelity does not lead into a concrete "religious" relationship with God. (Whether or not such a minimal relationship with the divine is existentially satisfactory is another question altogether.) Therefore, even if someone who recognizes God to be the source of his or her morality does in fact deceive me, I have something to hold up to that person, which is: why have you taken the name of your God in vain?

When it comes to a worshiper of the "mortal god" of Hobbes, it is hard to find any good reason for trust. Such a person can only be held to agreements that have been legally formalized, that is, agreements that have been concluded in a written document subject to the law of contracts, agreements whose violation can result in court proceedings to rectify the wrong. However, this assumes that there is no natural communality between persons wherein trust can be established.[82] When there is such communality, written contracts are only necessary either for the sake of clarity in complicated transactions or where the parties are total strangers one to the other. Only without any such communality do we need "the fear of the government, without which one person would swallow up another."[83] This is an ancient Jewish maxim that speaks of the imperial Rome which had conquered the Jews of Palestine. In a situation of political subjugation, one cannot assume that people have any other reason not to harm each other. In such a situation, order does not emerge from among trust among the people themselves; instead, order is imposed by an imperial conqueror, whom the people have to accept as at least something better than anarchy. However, it is not an order accepted rationally and freely, but one accepted out of fear of death or harsh punishment.

Even more profoundly, the Hobbesian situation is one where friendship is impossible. Yet as Aristotle pointed out, who would want to live without friends, even if he or she had everything else in life?[84] Along the same lines, an ancient sage is reported in the Talmud to have said, "Either friendship or death."[85] Friendship cannot endure where there is no trust, and how can there be trust if there is no standard to which persons are answerable both by themselves and with others? These standards "stand to reason," and they have long, overlapping traditions that indicate agreement about them. Hence this overlapping of traditions is neither contrived nor haphazard.

That is why, even though I might have to enter into a contractual agreement with such a person, one for whom nothing normative stands between him and the humanly instituted state, it is not something I would seek. In fact, I might well want to avoid it as much as possible. Even if I could be assured that the law will protect my interests that have been guaranteed by a written contract, such a person is not someone I would trust under any other circumstances. In other words, such a person is not someone I would want to be my friend. And even though only a very small percentage of the people I do business with in society are my friends, it would seem that if the vast majority of those who are not my friends could not be my friends under any circumstances, then such a society is a rather frightening place, no matter how many laws are on the books or no matter how well armed the police are.[86]

That is why the respectability of the state is not to initially rule where there has been anarchy heretofore but, rather, to enforce a law which is already in place in the more natural communities in which human beings live together long before they can agree to create anything new by contract. Edmund Burke stated it well: "[There are some duties] which are not in consequence of any special voluntary pact. They arise from the relation of man to God, which relations are not a matter of choice. On the contrary, the force of all the pacts which we enter into with any particular person, or number of persons . . . depends upon these prior obligations."[87] Indeed, when the state regards itself as the source of its own order, its own authority, it inevitably becomes more of a threat to the natural or human rights of its citizens—and beyond—than the individual criminals it is supposed to be protecting us from. One might well say that it is only when persons have already been uprooted from their natural communities that they are vulnerable enough to fearfully suppress their own rights and rush into the arms of the strange god of the Hobbesian state. Did we not see that with Hitler and Stalin—and others more recent?

One might well say that the reason our polities in Britain, the United States, and Canada (and others that have a connection to the biblically and philosophically informed morality epitomized by English Common Law) have not become Hobbesian-type tyrannies is because the majority of the citizens still believe themselves obligated by a prior, divine morality, despite the fact that most of them are unable to argue for it theoretically. That argumentation is the job of philosophers and theologians morally committed to our form of government. Only such prior obligation can make our human rights limit the power of the humanly created state, thus making it our servant, not our master.

Without such prior obligation and its protections, our human rights cannot trump the power of the state because they are derived from that very power, which without a true covenant standing over it, can easily take away what it has given.[88] So those who would interpret Grotius's dictum literally, that we can have law "even without God," and who claim that de facto atheism is the only cogent basis for commitment to a democratic polity, have no basis for rationally challenging the unjust exercise of state authority, which is the very antithesis of constitutional democracy. Ironically, those who cannot affirm either the cosmic order or the orderer of the cosmos have their human rights protected for them by the democratic commitments of those who have a moral religion or a religious morality. But how, then, can our doctrinaire secularists attempt to exclude, as they do more and more, their very protectors from the conversation any democracy needs to justify its own life and future?

Notes

1. Religious Liberty as a Political Claim

1. For the role the "Pilgrim Fathers" and their "Thanksgiving" celebration have played in the American imagination, see James Deetz and Patricia Scott Deetz, *The Times of Their Lives* (New York: W. H. Freeman and Co., 2000), 1–29.

2. See Karen Ordahl Kupperman, *The Jamestown Project* (Cambridge, MA: Harvard University Press, 2007), esp. 183–209.

3. See Francis Dillon, *A Place for Habitation* (London: Hutchinson and Co., 1973), 65–122.

4. See Everett Emerson, *Puritanism in America 1620–1750* (Boston: Twayne Publishers, 1977), 53–60; and Avihu Zakai, *Exile and Kingdom* (Cambridge: Cambridge University Press, 1992), 231–52. Cf. David Zaret, *The Heavenly Contract* (Chicago: University of Chicago Press, 1985), 128–36, 161–62.

5. See Timothy L. Hall, *Separating Church and State* (New York: Harcourt, Brace, and World, 1998), 152–66.

6. Richard John Neuhaus, *The Naked Public Square* (Grand Rapids, MI: Eerdmans Publishing Co., 1984), 20–37.

7. See Spinoza, *Tractatus Theologico-Politicus,* preface.

8. Philip Hamburger, *Separation of Church and State* (Cambridge, MA: Harvard University Press, 2002), 479–92. To my mind, this is the most learned and profound study of this topic to date.

9. See David Novak, *Covenantal Rights* (Princeton, NJ: Princeton University Press, 2000), 3–25.

10. Isaiah Berlin, "Two Concepts of Liberty," *Four Essays on Liberty* (Oxford: Oxford University Press, 1969), 122–31.

11. See Mary Ann Glendon, *Rights Talk* (New York: Free Press, 1991), 48–57.

12. Berlin, "Two Concepts of Liberty," 131–34.

13. See Aristotle, *Nicomachean Ethics* 1.1/1094ba1–10.

14. See Alasdair MacIntyre, *After Virtue* (Notre Dame, IN: University of Notre Dame Press, 1981), 169–209.

15. See David Novak, *The Jewish Social Contract* (Princeton, NJ: Princeton University Press, 2005), 10–21.

16. Maimonides, *Mishneh Torah:* Laws Concerning Murder 4.9.

17. See *Mishnah:* Yoma 8.9.

18. See Frank Barlow, *Thomas Becket* (London: Weidenfeld and Nicholson, 1986), 88–116.

19. See Ludwig Wittgenstein, *Philosophical Investigations,* 1.258–64.

20. See Jürgen Habermas, *Moral Consciousness and Communicative Action,* trans. C. Lenhardt and S. W. Nicholson (Cambridge, MA: MIT Press, 1993), 23–29.

21. See Aristotle, *Politics* 1.1/1253a9–19.

22. See John Rawls, *Political Liberalism* (New York: Columbia University Press, 1993). Cf. Novak, *The Jewish Social Contract,* 3, n. 6.

23. Immanuel Kant, *Religion within the Boundaries of Mere Reason,* trans. A. Wood and G. di Giovanni (Cambridge: Cambridge University Press, 1998), 108–10. (German text: *Die Religion innerhalb der Grenzen der blossen Vernunft,* Prussian Academy ed., 6:97–100.)

24. See Charlton T. Lewis and Charles Short, *A Latin Dictionary* (Oxford: Clarendon Press, 1962), 369–70, 488. Similarly, in Hebrew, the term *avodah* means "to attend to," be that the cultivation of the earth (see Gen. 2:15) or the cultivation of the covenantal relationship with God. See Marcus Jastrow, *A Dictionary of the Targumim* (New York: Pardes Publishing House, 1950), 1036. Similarly, in Greek, *leitourgia* means the same type of cultivation. See G. W. H. Lampe, *A Patristic Greek Lexicon* (Oxford: Clarendon Press, 1961), 795.

25. See Robert Bork, *The Tempting of America* (New York: Free Press, 1990), 113–14; also, *Slouching Towards Gomorrah* (New York: Harper Collins, 1996), 96–105.

26. For a full discussion of this whole issue, see *Sexual Orientation and Human Rights in American Religious Discourse,* ed. Saul M. Olyan and Martha C. Nussbaum (New York: Oxford University Press, 1998), esp.

Andrew Koppelman, "Sexual and Religious Pluralism," 215–33.

27. See David Novak, *Talking with Christians* (Grand Rapids, MI: Eerdmans, 2005), 184–202.

28. See *Encyclopedia Judaica,* 2nd ed., 3:692, s.v. "Herem de-Rabbenu Gershom."

29. See Novak, *The Jewish Social Contract,* 218–23.

30. See John Witte Jr., *From Sacrament to Contract* (Louisville, KY: Westminster John Knox Press, 1997), 177–219.

31. See David Michael Feldman, *Birth Control in Jewish Law* (New York: New York University Press, 1968), 46–59.

32. See David Novak, *Law and Theology in Judaism* (New York: KTAV, 1976), 60–63.

33. See *Babylonian Talmud:* Ketubot 11a.

34. Interestingly enough, in Jewish law an adopted child converted to Judaism by the request of the adoptive parents to a religious court, upon reaching his or her majority has the right to retroactively annul the conversion done on his or her behalf. That, certainly, is the adopted child's right to religious liberty. See ibid. See also David Novak, "The Legal Question of the Investigation of Converts," *Jewish Law Association Studies* III (Atlanta, GA: Scholars Press, 1987), 167–72. In this case, religious liberty means the right to confirm or repudiate a religious conversion conducted when one is incapable of free choice in the matter.

35. Plato, *Republic* 457b–466d; Aristotle, *Politics* 1261a1–1262b35.

36. See David Hume, *An Inquiry Concerning the Principles of Morals,* ed. C. W. Hendel (New York: Liberal Arts Press, 1957), 113–19.

2. Religious Liberty as a Philosophical Claim

1. See, e.g., David Novak, "Women in the Rabbinate?" *Halakhah in a Theological Dimension* (Chico, CA: Scholars Press, 1985), 61–71.

2. See infra, 89–99.

3. See Ps. 119:30–32; David Novak, *The Election of Israel* (Cambridge: Cambridge University Press, 1995), 143–52.

4. See *Babylonian Talmud:* Berakhot 4a re Ps. 27:13.

5. Ibid.: Yevamot 47b.

6. See David Novak, *Talking with Christians* (Grand Rapids, MI: Eerdmans, 2005), 127–45.

7. Thomas Aquinas *Summa Theologiae* 1, q. 2, a. 3, trans. L. Shapcote in *Basic Writings of Saint Thomas Aquinas* 1, ed. A. Pegis (New York:

Random House, 1945), 23. (Latin text, ed. P. Caramello [Rome: Marietti, 1962].)

8. See William David Ross, *Aristotle* (New York: Meridian Books, 1959), 175–82.

9. See Plato, *Phaedo* 97c–99b.

10. One can see how earthly nature when manifest in human appetites is not to be obeyed, but rather used in connection with the fulfillment of a commandment. See *Babylonian Talmud:* Kiddushin 30b re: Gen. 4:7.

11. See Yehezkel Kaufmann, *The Religion of Israel,* trans. M. Greenberg (Chicago: University of Chicago Press, 1960), 60–121.

12. John Finnis, *Natural Law and Natural Rights* (Oxford: Clarendon Press, 1980), 52. Cf. David Novak, *Covenantal Rights* (Princeton, NJ: Princeton University Press, 2000), 21–22.

13. See Hans Kelsen, *The Pure Theory of Law,* trans. M. Knight (Berkeley, CA: University of California Press, 1967), 221.

14. See Novak, *Talking with Christians,* 127–45.

15. Thus the Israeli jurist and rights theorist Haim H. Cohn writes in his book *Human Rights in Jewish Law*: "Speaking of human rights concepts I must say at once that no explicit concept of this kind is to be found in Jewish law. . . . It is mainly that the particular structure of Jewish law qua religious law—with God as the central object of love and veneration, and the worship and service of God as the overriding purpose of all law—postulates a system of duties rather than a system of rights" (New York: KTAV, 1984), 16–17.

16. Cf. *Babylonian Talmud:* Shevuot 30a–b.

17. Cf. ibid.: Baba Kama 38a re Hab. 3:6; David Novak, *The Image of the Non-Jew in Judaism* (New York and Toronto: Edwin Mellen Press, 1983), 60–64.

18. See Novak, *Covenantal Rights,* 3–12.

19. Anselm, *Proslogion* 2, trans. S. N. Deane, *St. Anslem: Basic Writings* (La Salle, IL: Open Court Publishing Co., 1962), 53–54.

20. See Novak, *Talking with Christians,* 108–26.

21. See David Novak, *Jewish Social Ethics* (New York: Oxford University Press, 1992), 232–34.

22. See ibid., 46–49.

23. In his *Metaphysics of Morals*, Kant argues that "children have by their procreation an original innate [*ursprünglich-angebornes*] (not acquired) [*nicht angeerbtes*] right to the care of their parents until they are able to look after themselves, and they have this right directly by law (*lege*), that is, without any special act being required to establish

[*erfordlich*] this right" (sec. 28 6:280), trans. M. Gregor (Cambridge: Cambridge University Press, 1996), 64). Nevertheless, without the prescription of the law, how would anyone be able to cogently assert that children do have this right as a right (*Recht*)? See *Babylonian Talmud:* Ketubot 49b. On the question of whether personal freedom (which, for Kant, *Metaphysic of Morals* [6:237], 30 is "the only original right belonging [*Zustehende Recht*] to every man by virtue of his humanity") is prior to one's being commanded or whether being commanded engenders one's personal freedom, see Maimonides *Mishneh Torah:* Laws Concerning Repentance 5.4; also, Hans Kelsen, *Pure Theory of Law*, trans. M. Knight (Berkeley, CA: University of California Press, 1970), 91–99.

24. When disassociating autonomy from any divine source, in his *Metaphysics of Morals*, Kant writes: "No concept can be formed of how it is possible for *God to create* free beings, for it seems as if all our future actions would have to be predetermined by that first act, included in the chain of natural causality [*Naturnothwendigkeit*] and therefore not free" (sec. 28 6:281, note thereon, 64). However, if we *receive* our freedom simultaneously when being commanded, ultimately if not yet immediately by God, then freedom comes from revelation (first general, then special), not from physical creation via natural causality. See *Babylonian Talmud:* Sanhedrin 56b re: Gen. 2:16 and 18:19; also, *Mishnah:* Avot 6.2 and *Babylonian Talmud:* Eruvin 54a re: Exod. 32:16. On the essential difference between normative speech and speech as exerting "causal influence," see Nicholas Wolterstorff, *Divine Discourse* (Cambridge: Cambridge University Press, 1995), 93.

25. Quoted in Emil L. Fackenheim, *To Mend the World* (New York: Schocken Books, 1982), 25, 217.

26. Ibid., 218.

27. Kant's rational prohibition of suicide could be seen as only extending to cases when I will my own death for the sensuous motive of avoiding physical or even emotional pain. See *Groundwork of the Metaphysics of Morals*, trans. H. J. Paton (New York: Harper and Row, 1964), 89. However, what if I want to kill myself because I have just been diagnosed with rapidly developing Alzheimer's disease and my dementia is imminent? Or, what if I were about to be dehumanized in a Nazi death camp and, therefore, I want to die with my rationality intact? In these cases, were I to kill myself, my motive would not be sensuous; rather, it would be for the sake of my rationality, which Kant takes to be coequal with my nature, with my human dignity (see ibid., 102–03). Certainly, my intact human dignity is an end in itself (see ibid., 95–99). Wouldn't my

killing myself, then, be an affirmation of my dignity? Or in the latter case, could one say that this would be cooperating with those who were trying to dehumanize me, hence it would be an assault on my dignity? (This very question was posed to me at my defense of my Ph.D. dissertation, part of which was on Kant's treatment of suicide, in the Department of Philosophy of Georgetown University on March 23, 1971.) Kant, no doubt, would have called this a "casuistical question," viz., a question to which his ethical system provides no clear-cut answer. See Kant, *The Metaphysical Principle of Virtue*, 6:422-24, trans. J. Ellington (Indianapolis: Bobbs-Merrill, 1964), 82–85; also, H. J. Paton, *The Categorical Imperative* (Chicago: University of Chicago Press, 1948), 171; and the subsequent publication of my Ph.D. dissertation, *Suicide and Morality* (New York: Scholars Studies Press, 1975), 104–07.

28. See Baruch Spinoza, *Ethics*, 3.P6–10; Henri Bergson, *Creative Evolution*, trans. A. Mitchell (New York: Random House, 1944), 57–58.

29. See Sigmund Freud, *Beyond the Pleasure Principle*, trans. J. Strachey (New York: Bantam Books, 1959), 70–78.

30. Karl Barth, *Church Dogmatics*, 2/2.8 (Edinburgh: T. & T. Clark, 1957), 651.

31. See David Novak, *Jewish-Christian Dialogue* (New York: Oxford University Press, 1989), 148–51.

32. Barth, *Church Dogmatics*, 667.

33. See David Novak, *Talking with Christians* (Grand Rapids, MI: Eerdmans, 2005), 127–45.

34. See *Babylonian Talmud:* Sanhedrin 56b re Gen. 2:16 (concerning the prohibition of bloodshed).

35. See Immanuel Kant, *Critique of Practical Reason*, 5:125–26, trans. W. S. Pluhar (Indianapolis: Bobbs-Merrill, 2002), 159.

36. Ibid., 5:132, p. 167.

37. Alan Dershowitz, *America Declares Independence* (Hoboken, NJ: John Wiley and Sons, 2003), 100.

38. See Kant, *Critique of Pure Reason*, B669.

39. Ibid., 115–16.

40. See Novak, *Covenantal Rights*, 166–72.

41. See David Michael Feldman, *Birth Control in Jewish Law* (New York: New York University Press, 1968), 56–59.

42. See David Novak, *The Sanctity of Human Life* (Washington, D.C.: Georgetown University Press, 2007), 5.

43. Cf. Emmanuel Levinas, "Ideology and Idealism," trans. S. Ames and A. Lesley, *The Levinas Reader*, ed. S. Hand (Oxford: Basil Blackwell, 1989), 246–47.

3. Religious Liberty as a Theological Claim

1. Spinoza, *Tractatus Theologico-Politicus*, trans. S. Shirley (Leiden: E. J. Brill, 1991), chap. 20, 232.
2. See Michel Vovelle, *1793: La révolution contre l'église* (Brussels: Éditions Complexe, 1988), 25–44.
3. Robert Cover, "Obligation: A Jewish Jurisprudence of the Social Order," *Journal of Law and Religion* 5 (1987), 65–74. Cf. David Novak, *Covenantal Rights* (Princeton, NJ: Princeton University Press, 2000), 27–32.
4. See Ceslas Spicq, *Theological Lexicon of the New Testament* 3, trans. J. D. Ernest (Peabody, MA: Hendrickson Publishers, 1994), 406–13, s.v. "hypokrisis."
5. See Isa. 2:1–4; Zech. 14:1–9.
6. See *Babylonian Talmud:* Berakhot 34b re Isa. 64:3.
7. See Clifford Geertz, *The Interpretation of Cultures* (New York: Basic Books, 1973), 5–30. See also, G. W. F. Hegel, *Phenomenology of Spirit,* trans. A. V. Miller (Oxford: Oxford University Press, 1977), 268–71; *Philosophy of Right,* nos. 135, 153–56, trans. T. M. Knox (Oxford: Clarendon Press, 1952), 89–90, 109–10.
8. See David Novak, *The Jewish Social Contract* (Princeton, NJ: Princeton University Press, 2000), 65–70.
9. *Babylonian Talmud:* Shabbat 88a re Exod. 19:17.
10. Aristotle, *Nicomachean Ethics* 3.3/1112a18–1113a12.
11. Shakespeare, *Hamlet,* 3.1.56.
12. *Babylonian Talmud:* Shabbat 88a.
13. Ibid. See Novak, *The Jewish Social Contract,* 70–77.
14. Maimonides, *Mishneh Torah:* Laws Concerning Repentance 5.1–5.
15. See *Mishnah:* Kiddushin 1.9.
16. Aristotle, *Nicomachean Ethics* 1.3/1095a5–10.
17. Kant, *Groundwork of the Metaphysic of Morals,* trans. H. J. Paton (New York: Harper and Row, 1964), 4:405, p. 73.
18. See Nietzsche, *The Will to Power,* 251, trans. W. Kaufmann and R. J. Hollingdale (New York: Vintage Books, 1968), 144–45.
19. See David Weiss Halivni, *Revelation Restored* (Boulder, CO: Westview Press, 1997), 82–85.
20. *Babylonian Talmud:* Yoma 69b re: Zech. 5:8.
21. See *Babylonian Talmud:* Avodah Zarah 36a and parallels.
22. See *Avot de-Rabbi Nathan,* chap. 34; *Bemidbar Rabbah* 3.13 re: Deut. 29:28; *Babylonian Talmud:* Menahot 45a.
23. Jürgen Habermas, *Moral Consciousness and Communicative Action,*

trans. C. Lenhardt and S. W. Nicholsen (Cambridge, MA: MIT Press, 1990), 200–203.

24. See *Babylonian Talmud:* Pesahim 66a–b.

25. See *Babylonian Talmud:* Menahot 89a. Cf. *Sifre:* Bemidbar 75, ed. Horovitz, p. 70 re Num. 10:8.

26. *Palestinian Talmud:* Peah 7.6/20c; *Babylonian Talmud:* Berakhot 45a and parallels.

27. See *Babylonian Talmud:* Eruvin 13b; also, *Tosefta:* Terumot 3.12.

28. See Maimonides, *Mishneh Torah:* Laws Concerning Rebels 2.7 and Joseph Karo, *Kesef Mishneh* thereon.

29. See *Babylonian Talmud:* Eruvin 68b; *Babylonian Talmud:* Baba Batra 31b and Rashbam, s.v. "le-zeiluta."

30. See *Mishnah:* Eduyot 1.5–6; also, *Babylonian Talmud:* Shabbat 112b.

31. See *Babylonian Talmud:* Shabbat 23a re Deut. 17:12; *Babylonian Talmud:* Avodah Zarah 35a; *Babylonian Talmud:* Yevamot 89a.

32. See David Novak, *Natural Law in Judaism* (Cambridge: Cambridge University Press, 1998), 92–121.

33. See Maimonides, *Mishneh Torah:* Laws Concerning Rebels 2.7 and Joseph Karo, *Kesef Mishneh* thereon.

34. *Babylonian Talmud:* Avodah Zarah 36a and parallels.

35. Ibid.

36. *Mishnah:* Eduyot 1.5.

37. See Maimonides, *Mishneh Torah:* Laws Concerning Rebels 2.7 and Joseph Karo, *Kesef Mishneh* thereon. Cf. *Babylonian Talmud:* Avodah Zarah 36a and Rashi, s.v. "lo pashat." Re: permitted omission, see *Babylonian Talmud:* Yevamot 90b.

38. *Babylonian Talmud:* Baba Batra 60b and *Tosafot,* s.v. "mutav."

39. See David Novak, *The Election of Israel* (Cambridge: Cambridge University Press, 1995), 189–99.

40. *Babylonian Talmud:* Baba Kama 28b re Deut. 22:26.

41. See *Babylonian Talmud:* Sanhedrin 74a–b.

42. See *Babylonian Talmud:* Kiddushin 49b.

43. Ibid. 68b re Deut. 7:4.

44. *Mishnah:* Avot 4.22.

45. *Mishnah:* Sanhedrin 10.1; Maimonides, *Mishneh Torah:* Laws Concerning Kings 8.11; *Tosefta:* Sanhedrin 13.2 and *Babylonian Talmud:* Sanhedrin 105a re Ps. 9:18.

46. Maimonides, *Mishneh Torah:* Laws Concerning Kings 8.10.

47. *Babylonian Talmud:* Ketubot 11a. See, also, *Babylonian Talmud:* Hullin 3b and *Tosafot,* s.v. "qe-savar"; *Babylonian Talmud:* Yevamot 24b and *Tosafot,* s.v. "halakhah."

48. See *Babylonian Talmud:*. Yevamot 22a and parallels; also, ibid. 24b.

49. See *Babylonian Talmud:* Keritot 9a.

50. *Babylonian Talmud:* Yevamot 47b.

51. See *Babylonian Talmud:* Baba Kama 42a and parallels. Cf. *Tanhuma:* Tsav re Ps. 65:5, ed. Buber, 9b–10a.

52. See Jacob Katz, *Halakhah ve-Kabbalah* (Jerusalem: Magnes Press, 1986), 255–69.

53. *Babylonian Talmud:* Sanhedrin 44a re Josh. 7:11.

54. *Teshuvot Rashi* 171, ed. Elfenbein, 191–93. But in his commentary on *Babylonian Talmud:* Sanhedrin 44a (s.v. "hata yisrael"), Rashi interprets *yisrael* to mean the Jewish people, i.e., collective Israel, which is clearly the meaning of both the biblical and talmudic texts.

55. See *Sifre:* Bemidbar 111 re: Num. 15:22, ed. Horovitz, 116; *Sifre:* Devarim 54 re Deut. 11:28, ed. Finkelstein, 122, fn. 9.

56. *Mishnah:* Gittin 4.9; *Babylonian Talmud:* Gittin 46b–47a; *Tur:* Yoreh Deah 252.

57. *Babylonian Talmud:* Gittin 47a. Also, see *Babylonian Talmud:* Shabbat 68a.

58. See Novak, *The Election of Israel,* 196–97.

59. See David Novak, *Talking with Christians* (Grand Rapids, MI: Eerdmans, 2005), 146–66.

60. *Mishnah:* Avot 6.2 re Exod. 32:16.

61. Note *Thus Spake Zarathustra,* 2: "The holy man answered, 'I make songs and sing them; and when I make songs, I do laugh, weep, and mumble: so do I praise God. . . . But when Zarathustra was alone, so did he speak in his heart: 'Could this then be possible! This old holy man in his forest has not yet heard that God is dead [*Gott tot ist*]!'" (my translation) German text, *Friedrich Nietzsche: Werke* I (Munich: Carl Hanser Verlag, 1967), 548–49.

62. See Plato, *Republic* 409c–e.

4. Religious Liberty in a Secular Society

1. The most influential proponent of the privatization of religion in a secular democratic society is still the late Leo Pfeffer (d. 1993), who for many years was legal counsel to the American Jewish Congress, and who argued some of the most important church-state cases before the U.S. Supreme Court in the mid-twentieth century. See, for example, *Church, State, and Freedom,* rev. ed. (Boston: Beacon Press, 1967), 3.

2. William James, *The Varieties of Religious Experience* (New York: Mentor Books, 1958), 42.

3. Sarah Schmidt, [headline of article], *National Post and Opinion,* May 18, 2002, B1.

4. See Garry Wills, *Inventing America* (Garden City, NY: Doubleday, 1978), 213–15.

5. See Isaiah Berlin, "Two Concepts of Liberty," *Four Essays on Liberty* (New York: Oxford University Press, 1969), 121–31; Louis D. Brandeis, "The Right to Privacy," quoted in Mary Ann Glendon, *Rights Talk* (New York: Free Press, 1991), 47; also see ibid. 47–75.

6. Schmidt.

7. Ibid.

8. Thomas Aquinas, *Summa Theologiae* 1–2, q. 90, a. 1.

9. Moses Maimonides, *Mishneh Torah: Laws Concerning Kings* 10.9.

10. See Immanuel Kant, *Groundwork of the Metaphysic of Morals*, trans. H. J. Paton (New York: Harper and Row, 1964), 65–68.

11. See David Novak, *Talking with Christians* (Grand Rapids, MI: Eerdmans Publishing Co., 2005), 116–17.

12. See David Novak, *The Jewish Social Contract* (Princeton, NJ: Princeton University Press, 2005), 12–21.

13. See David Novak, *Natural Law in Judaism* (Cambridge: Cambridge University Press, 1998), 62–72.

14. For the sources of this teaching, see Louis Ginzberg, *Legends of the Jews* 5 (Philadelphia: Jewish Publication Society of America, 1925), 137–38, n. 16.

15. *Babylonian Talmud:* Berakhot 34b re Isa. 64:3. Also, see 1 Cor. 2:9.

5. God and Human Rights: A Biblical-Talmudic Perspective

1. Ronald Dworkin, *Taking Rights Seriously* (Cambridge: Harvard University Press, 1978), 205.

2. See Glendon, *Rights Talk,* 47–89.

3. The term *theocracy* (literally, "the rule of God") was coined by the first-century Jewish historian Josephus, who said it means "placing all sovereignty [*archē*] and authority in the hands of God" (*Against Apion,* 2.167, trans. H. St.-John Thackeray [Cambridge, MA: Harvard University Press, 1926], 1:358–59). Josephus is referring to a Jewish society ruled according to revealed law. Yet, even in such a society, one can recognize the two features of democracy most of us hold dear, namely, popularly chosen government and human rights. Moreover, as I shall

argue later, even secular societies like the United States and Canada, which are not governed by revealed law, might be considered "theocracies" inasmuch as they recognize in their founding documents that all rights, including the right of popularly chosen government, are from God. Unfortunately, though, the term "theocracy" is now frequently used to designate such antidemocratic states as Iran and Saudi Arabia, which are governed by dictatorships dominated by clerics.

4. See David Novak, *The Jewish Social Contract* (Princeton, NJ: Princeton University Press, 2005).

5. Unless otherwise noted, all biblical quotations in English are my own translation from the traditional (Masoretic) texts: *Biblia Hebraica*, seventh ed., ed. R. Kittel (Stuttgart, 1951).

6. *Mekhilta:* Neziqin, trans. J. Z. Lauterbach (Philadelphia: Jewish Publication Society of America, 1935), 3:141.

7. I translate the first sentence in the vocative voice rather than in the interrogative voice (as in most of the English translations), following Martin Buber and Franz Rosenzweig's German translation: *Was hast du getan! (Die Fünf Bücher der Weisung)* (Cologne: Jakob Hegner, 1954), 18.

8. See David Novak, *Halakhah in a Theological Dimension* (Chico, CA: Scholars Press, 1985), 96–101; also, David Novak, *Natural Law in Judaism* (Cambridge: Cambridge University Press, 1998), 167–73.

9. See *Babylonian Talmud:* Zevahim 116a (the view of Rabbi Joshua).

10. See *Babylonian Talmud:* Baba Kama 99b–100a re Exod. 18:20, where the practice of equity is prescribed in cases where following the strict sense of positive law would lead to great injustice in fact. See, for example, *Babylonian Talmud:* Baba Metsia 83a re Prov. 2:20.

11. *Babylonian Talmud:* Baba Kama 93a re Gen. 16:5 and Tosafot, s.v. "d'eeka" thereon; also, Nahmanides, *Commentary on the Torah:* Exod. 22:22.

12. In *Midrash ha-Gadol:* it is Cain who, during a fight with his brother, pleads for his life from Abel, but when Abel releases him, he then treacherously turns on Abel and kills him on the spot. The implication here is that Abel would also have pleaded with Cain for his life if he had had the chance to do so (Genesis, ed. M. Margulies (Jerusalem: Mosad ha-Rav Kook, 1947), 119), Cf. Louis Ginzberg, *The Legends of the Jews* (Philadelphia: Jewish Publication Society of America, 1909–28), 1:109.

13. See Novak, *Jewish Social Ethics*, 163–65.

14. W. H. Auden, "September 1, 1939," in *Seven Centuries of Verse: English and American,* second revised ed., ed. A. J. M. Smith (New York: Charles Scribner's Sons, 1957), 686.

15. See *Babylonian Talmud:* Nedarim 11a and parallels.

16. *Babylonian Talmud:* Shabbat 31a.

17. This fundamental denial is put in the mouth of Cain by the rabbis. See *Targum Yerushalmi:* Gen. 4:8; also, *Palestinian Talmud:* Kiddushin 4.1/65b.

18. See *Babylonian Talmud:* Sanhedrin 109a–b; also, Ginzberg, *The Legends of the Jews,* 1:245–50.

19. See *Palestinian Talmud:* Sanhedrin 2.3/20a re Ps. 17:2.

20. See *Babylonian Talmud:* Taanit 16a re Jonah 3:8; also, Ginzberg, *The Legends of the Jews,* 4:250–53.

21. See *Babylonian Talmud:* Sanhedrin 54a.

22. Cf. Exod. 2:14.

23. See, for example, Deut. 29:22–23; Isa. 1:9.

24. *Tosefta:* Sanhedrin 13.8.

25. See supra, 33–37, 44–49.

6. The Human Rights of the "Other" in Jewish Tradition

1. See, e.g., *Babylonian Talmud:* Baba Kama 57a; *Palestinian Talmud:* Baba Kama 10.1/7b. In rabbinic Hebrew, such a claimant is called a *to'en*; the one being so claimed is called a *nit'an*. Another pair of terms for the right-duty relation is *tove'ah* and *nitb'a* or *tevu'ah* (see *Mishnah:* Ketubot 5.2; *Babylonian Talmud:* Ketubot 57a–b). A third pair of terms is *zak'ai* and *hayyav* (see *Mishnah:* Sanhedrin 3.6; 4.1). Understanding how these pairs of terms operate in rabbinic legal and theological texts should dispel the mistaken notion that the Jewish tradition has no concept of rights as we now understand that term. Furthermore, our word "right" as in *human rights* might very well be based on the Latin *iustus,* by which the Vulgate translates the Hebrew *tsaddiq,* meaning someone who has been justified in his or her innocence of legal wrongdoing (see Gen. 18:25). Along these lines, see Brian Tierney, *The Idea of Natural Rights* (Atlanta, GA: Scholars Press, 1997), 343. For the notion of rights as *just deserts,* see Lenn Evan Goodman, *On Justice* (New Haven, CT: Yale University Press, 1991), 23–42.

2. See David Novak, *Covenantal Rights* (Princeton, NJ: Princeton University Press,) 3–32.

3. See Isaiah Berlin, "Two Concepts of Liberty," in *Four Essays on Liberty* (Oxford: Oxford University Press, 1969), 122–41.

4. See Aristotle *Politics* 1.1/1253a1–30. Cf. Gen. 2:18–24.

25

5. See Cicero, *De Republica* 3.2.3, *De Legibus* 1.7.23 and 1.15.42.

6. See Gen. 1:27, 5:1, 9:6.

7. See *Babylonian Talmud:* Sanhedrin 56b re Gen. 2:16 and 18:19.

8. See Joseph Albo, *Book of Principles,* 1.8, trans. I. Husik (Philadelphia: Jewish Publication Society of America, 1929), 1:80–92.

9. See supra, 108–16.

10. See *Babylonian Talmud:* Sanhedrin 24b; Maimonides, *Mishneh Torah:* Laws Concerning Murderers 4.9.

11. See Rashi, *Commentary on the Torah:* Gen. 4:9.

12. See *Babylonian Talmud:* Sanhedrin 54a.

13. See Gen. 20:1; Exod. 1:17.

14. See *Palestinian Talmud:* Nedarim 9.3/14c re Lev. 19:18 and Gen. 5:1; *Mishnah:* Avot 3.14 and the commentary thereon of Barukh Halevi Epstein, *Barukh She'amar* (Tel Aviv: Am Olam, 1965), 121–22.

15. *Mishnah:* Ketubot 9.3.

16. *Babylonian Talmud:* Sanhedrin 72a re Exod. 22:1.

17. *Palestinian Talmud:* Sotah 9.6/23d re Deut. 21:7.

18. Plato, *Philebus* 60a–e; Aristotle, *Nicomachean Ethics* 10.2/1173b25–1174a13.

19. See Emmanuel Levinas, "The Rights of Man and the Rights of the Other," *Outside the Subject,* trans. M. B. Smith (Stanford, CA: Stanford University Press, 1994), 116–25.

20. See Arthur A. Cohen, *Tremendum* (New York: Crossroad, 1981).

21. See Deut. 7:6–8.

22. See Exod. 22:20 and 23:9; Lev. 19:33–34; Deut. 10:19. Cf. *Babylonian Talmud:* Baba Kama 38a; also, Novak, *The Image of the Non-Jew in Judaism,* 60–64.

23. See *Babylonian Talmud:* Kiddushin 40b.

24. See ibid.: Arakhin 29a.

25. See Maimonides, *Mishneh Torah:* Law Concerning Forbidden Intercourse 14.8. Cf. note of Abraham ben David (Ravad) thereon.

26. *Babylonian Talmud:* Avodah Zarah 64b.

27. Maimonides, *Mishneh Torah:* Laws Concerning Kings 9.1. Cf. *Babylonian Talmud:* Sanhedrin 57a.

28. *Tosefta:* Avodah Zarah 8.4–6.

29. See, e.g., Marvin Fox, "Maimonides and Aquinas on Natural Law," *Interpreting Maimonides* (Chicago: University of Chicago Press, 1990), 130–43.

30. See David Novak, *Natural Law in Judaism* (Cambridge: Cambridge University Press, 1998).

31. See *Babylonian Talmud:* Shabbat 128b; Baba Metsia 32b re Exod. 23:5.

32. See Maimonides *Mishneh Torah:* Laws Concerning Kings 8.9–10.

33. See David Novak, *Jewish-Christian Dialogue* (Grand Rapids, MI: Eerdmans, 2005), 26–56.

34. Thus adult children are to resist the illegitimate claims of their parents on them in the name of the higher, justifiable claim of God on both of them. See *Babylonian Talmud:* Yevamot 5b (and *Tosafot,* s.v. "kulkhem" thereon), also, ibid.: Sotah 11b re Exod. 1:17.

35. See ibid.: Yevamot 79a–b.

36. *Tosefta:* Gittin 3.14; *Babylonian Talmud:* Gittin 61a.

37. Maimonides, *Mishneh Torah:* Laws Concerning Kings 8.9–10.

38. Nahmanides, *Commentary on the Torah:* Gen. 34:14. Cf. Maimonides *Mishneh Torah:* Laws Concerning Kings 9.14. See Novak, *Jewish Social Ethics,* 189–96.

39. See David Novak, "Land and People: One Jewish Perspective" in *Boundaries and Justice,* ed. D. Miller and S. H. Hashmi (Princeton, NJ: Princeton University Press, 2001), 213–36.

40. Hermann Cohen, *Religion of Reason Out of the Sources of Judaism,* trans. S. Kaplan (New York: Frederick Ungar, 1972), 122–32.

41. Maimonides, *Mishneh Torah:* Laws Concerning Kings 8.10.

42. See David Novak, *The Image of the Non-Jew in Judaism* (New York: Edwin Mellen Press, 1983), 96–99.

43. See ibid., 14–19.

44. See Novak, *Jewish-Christian Dialogue,* 42–72. At this point, it is worth noting that in the Bible itself, in marked difference from many rabbinic texts, there does not seem to be a prohibition of polytheism, with or without idols, to gentiles. There the prohibition of "other gods" is only made to Israel who, quite uniquely, is covenanted to the One and Only God, a relationship often compared to an interminable, monogamous marriage.

45. See Novak, *The Image of the Non-Jew in Judaism,* 130–38.

46. See, e.g., Plato, *Laws* 716c; Cicero, *De Legibus* 1.7.23.

7. Law: Religious or Secular?

1. The rabbinic admonition to judges to "be deliberate [*metunim*] in judgment" (*Mishnah:* Avot 1.1) can mean determining whether a case calls for ordinary, concise legal debate, or extraordinary, prolonged legal debate. See *Tosefta:* Hagigah 2.9 and Sanhedrin 7.1. The rabbinic admonition about "delaying judgment" (*innui ha-din*) applies to the needless prolongation of ordinary legal debate. See *Mishnah:* Avot 5.8;

Babylonian Talmud: Shabbat 33a and Rashi, s.v. "innui ha-din."

2. James Davison Hunter, *Culture Wars* (New York: Basic Books, 1991), esp., chapter 4.

3. Hans Kelsen, *The Pure Theory of Law,* trans. M. Knight (Berkeley, CA: University of California Press, 1970), 8–10, 193–95.

4. See Aristotle, *Nicomachean Ethics* 5.1/1129b26.

5. See note 3, chap. 5.

6. See Stephen L. Carter, *The Culture of Disbelief* (New York: Anchor Books, 1994), 4.

7. See Kant, *Groundwork of the Metaphysic of Morals,* trans. H. J. Paton (New York: Harper and Row, 1964), 69–71.

8. See Plato, *Laws* 885c–d.

9. The biblical name *elohim,* for the Rabbis, almost always designates both God as supreme authority and human judge as exercising authority when they properly adjudicate based on the divine law. See *Beresheet Rabbah* 33.3; *Shemot Rabbah* 3.6 re Exod. 3:14; *Babylonian Talmud:* Sanhedrin 56b; ibid. 6b re Ps. 82:1 and 2 Chron. 19:6; ibid. 66a re Exod. 22:27; also, Arthur Marmorstein, *The Old Rabbinic Doctrine of God* (Oxford: Oxford University Press, 1927), 43–53.

10. See Plato *Laws* 889e–890a; also, J. W. Gough, *The Social Contract,* 2nd ed. (Oxford: Clarendon Press, 1957), 11–15.

11. Grotius, *The Rights of War and Peace,* Prol. XI, trans. John Morrice [1715], ed. R. Tuck (Indianapolis: Liberty Fund, 2005), 89.

12. Ibid., 91.

13. Along the lines of what has now been called a "hermeneutic of suspicion," see Leo Strauss, *Persecution and the Art of Writing* (Gleoncoe, IL: Free Press, 1952), 22–37.

14. See Kant, *Critique of Pure Reason,* B637.

15. See Leo Strauss, *Natural Right and History* (Chicago: University of Chicago Press, 1953), 146.

16. *Babylonian Talmud:* Kiddushin 42a and parallels.

17. Plato, *Euthyphro* 10a (my translation). Greek text, rev. ed. C. E. Graves (London: Macmillan, 1952).

18. Ibid., 12d.

19. Plato, *Republic* 509b.

20. Sophocles, *Antigione* 59–65, 173–74, 449–57.

21. The problem with a merely procedural notion of natural law, such as that of the American legal theorist Lon L. Fuller in *The Morality of Law,* rev. ed. (New Haven and London: Yale University Press, 1969), 96–106, is that it only provides a criterion of inner coherence for a legal system, that is, *how* it is to operate well. But surely *why* one should obey any

body of law requires more of a reason than that its system is internally consistent.

22. See Plato, *Laws* 899d, *Phaedrus* 248a, *Symposium* 202e, *Theaetetus* 176a–b, *Timaeus* 68e–69a.

23. Cicero, *De Legibus* 1.7.23, trans. C. W. Keynes (Cambridge, MA: Harvard University Press, 1928), 320–23.

24. Aristotle, *Metaphysics* 12.8/1072b20–30 and 1074b1–4.

25. See Aristotle, *Nicomachean Ethics* 5.7/1134b20–34.

26. See Plato, *Timaeus* 29e–30d; *Republic* 500c–d; *Laws* 624a, 713c.

27. The quintessential expression of nondivine, purely human authority is the dictum of the sophist Protagoras that "man is the measure [*metron*] of all things useful [*pantōn chrēmatōn*]" (Plato *Theatetus* 152a, *Cratylus* 386a). The term *to chrēmatos* ("useful thing") comes from *cheir,* the word for hand, that is, something humans can manipulate or construct by means of *technē,* what we would now call "technique" (see Aristotle, *Nicomachean Ethics* 6.4/1140a1–20). The question this human activity needs to ask itself regularly is whether the criterion by which and for which it makes such things as laws is of its own making or is it something this human activity receives from what is higher and more permanent than itself. Cf. Plato, *Laws* 716c.

28. Plato, *Laws* 713c, trans. R. G. Bury (Cambridge, Mass.: Harvard University Press, 1926), 284–87.

29. Ronald Dworkin, *Law's Empire* (Cambridge, MA: Belknap Press, 1986), 407: "The courts are the capitals of law's empire, and judges are its princes, but not its seers and prophets. It falls to philosophers, if they are willing, to work out law's ambitions for itself, the purer form of law within and beyond the law we have." Cf. Plato, *Republic* 473d.

30. See, e.g., A. P. d'Entrèves, *Natural Law: An Historical Survey* (New York: Harper and Row, 1965).

31. In his notes to Grotius's text, which were translated into English from the French in John Morrice's translation of *De jure belli ac pacis* (see n. 11 above), Jean Barbeyrac comments (Prol. XII, p. 90, n. 1): "In Reality, he is here talking of *Voluntary Divine Law,* as he himself calls it [1.1.15] . . . for he calls the Will, which is the Source of this Right, a free or arbitrary *Will;* and afterwards observes, as it were occasionally, that the *Law of Nature,* of which he has been laying the Foundation, may also be considered as flowing from the Divine Will. . . . But it may be further said that the Law of Nature, though sufficiently founded in itself, does likewise derive its Origin from God, independently of Revelation. . . . Many Pagan Authors have also acknowledged that the Law of Nature is a divine law."

32. See Plato, *Timaeus* 29e–30c.

33. Tertullian, *De Praescriptione Haereticorum* 7. See Harry Austryn Wolfson, *The Philosophy of the Church Fathers*, 3rd rev. ed. (Cambridge, MA: Harvard University Press, 1956), 102–11. Tertullian's view is hardly uniquely Christian; a number of significant Jewish theologians said virtually the same thing. See David Novak, *The Theology of Nahmanides Systematically Presented* (Atlanta, GA: Scholars Press, 1992), 56–58. For some recent Catholic attempts to reemphasize the theological foundations of natural law, see Russell Hittinger, *The First Grace: Rediscovering the Natural Law in a Post-Christian World* (Wilmington, DE: ISI Books, 2003), and Matthew Levering, *Biblical Natural Law* (Oxford: Oxford University Press, 2008).

34. See note 29 above. Cf. Karl Popper, *The Open Society and Its Enemies*, 2 vols. (Princeton, NJ: Princeton University Press, 1950), *passim*.

35. See Kant, *Critique of Pure Reason*, B67–72.

36. This principle has been interpreted in a variety of ways during the history of Judaism. See David Novak, "The Idea of Natural Law in the Thought of Hermann Cohen" (Heb.) in *Jubilee Volume for David Weiss Halivni* [Heb. sec.] (Jerusalem: Orhot Press, 2004), 131, n. 2. My use of it here reflects the notion that the Torah is capable of being translated into any human language (see, e.g., *Tosefta: Sotah* 8.6; *Babylonian Talmud: Sotah* 35b re Deut. 27:8). Cf. Ludwig Wittgenstein, *Tractatus Logico-Philosophicus*, 3.03–3.032; 5.6–5.62; *Philosophical Investigations* I, no. 23.

37. When Leo Strauss questioned the "typically modern dualism of a nonteleological natural science and a teleological science of man" (*Natural Right and History*, 8), he ignores Kantian and Hegelian efforts to build an ethical-political program of human perfectability within History rather than within Nature. Nevertheless, it is questionable whether this kind of philosophical idealism can save human purposiveness when human striving is put back into Nature by Darwinian biology, which demonstrates that the striving of any living being is limited to striving for the survival of its species. But such a blind drive requires neither consciousness nor will when being ascribed to Nature or any of its parts, hence it allows for nothing that had heretofore been considered uniquely human. Hence in order for human purposiveness to remain ontologically cogent, it needs an ontology in which humans are taken to be the pinnacle of all creation.

38. One finds, however a hint of this in Plato's *Republic* 473d: "Until philosophers will exercise kingship [*basileusōsin*] in the cities, or those now called kings and potentates will do philosophy [*philosophēsōsi*], . . .

there will be no rest from evils for the cities, nor do I think for human-kind [*tō anthrōpinō genei*], nor will this very republic [*hautē hē politeia*] come forth . . ." (my translation). In other words, Plato hints that his optimal human polity must be conceived as having universal potential (*eis to dynaton*). Cf. ibid., 540d.

39. See e.g. *Babylonian Talmud:* Sanhedrin 97b re Hab. 2:3; Maimonides, *Mishneh Torah: Laws About Kings* 12.2.

40. Thus Pharaoh, whose self-acknowledgment of his own divine status was noted (though ridiculed) by the Bible (e.g. Ezek. 29:9), challenges the divine authority of the God of Israel to command him to release this putative god's supposed subjects (see Exod. 5:2 and commentary of Abraham ibn Ezra thereon). The assumption in this very plausible chal-lenge is that Pharaoh would only obey someone generically superior to himself, but not even someone of his own divine genus, let alone a being whose divinity has yet to be demonstrated. A major point of the whole Exodus narrative is that the God of Israel forces Pharaoh to accept his generic superiority (see ibid., 8:6; 12:12), even though that fact "hardens Pharaoh's heart" (see ibid., 7:14; 8:15), that is, forces Pharaoh to accept in praxis what he could not accept in theory. Furthermore, the same is-sue seems to be at stake when Athens accuses Socrates of serving "new gods" (Plato *Euthyphro* 3b). But Socrates' justification of his philosophi-cal activities based on the command of a god (Plato, *Apology* 23a) falls on deaf ears inasmuch as the Athenian authorities do not recognize the divinity whose command Socrates claims to be following (ibid., 24b).

41. *Babylonian Talmud:* Rosh Hashanah 4b.

42. See David Novak, *Natural Law in Judaism* (Cambridge: Cambridge University Press, 1998), 27–61.

43. See note 9 above.

44. See *Babylonian Talmud:* Pesahim 87b re Prov. 8:22.

45. See David Novak, *Covenantal Rights* (Princeton, NJ: Princeton Uni-versity Press, 2000), 3–32.

46. See David Novak, *The Election of Israel* (Cambridge: Cambridge University Press, 1995), 126–27.

47. In the Bible, *derekh erets* refers to natural human mortality (see Josh. 23:14; 1 Kings 2:2). For the rabbis, the term means how mortal humans in general are to positively construct a world with a minimum of destruction (see, e.g., *Mishnah: Avot* 3.17; *Vayiqra Rabbah* 9.3 re Gen. 3:24; *Babylonian Talmud:* Yoma 69b).

48. See David Novak, *Covenantal Rights* (Princeton, NJ: Princeton Uni-versity Press, 2000), 142–52.

49. See Strauss, *Natural Right and History*, 120–64.

50. See Plato *Republic* 501b–c.

51. See *Babylonian Talmud:* Yevamot 22a; *Babylonian Talmud:* Sanhedrin 59b; also, *Mishnah:* Baba Metsia 7.11.

52. Along these lines, see *Palestinian Talmud:* Megillah 1.7/70d re Deut. 5:19; also, *Tosefta:* Berakhot 1.12 re Jer. 23:7–8.

53. Quoted in John Witte Jr., "Blest Be the Ties That Bind: Covenant and Community in Puritan Thought," *Emory Law Journal* 36 (1987), 579. See also Witte, *The Reformation of Rights* (Cambridge: Cambridge University Press, 2007), 277–319.

54. See Strauss, *Natural Right and History,* 119.

55. Plato, *Republic* 331e (my translation).

56. Originally from *Ulpian Digest* 1.1.10.1.

57. Thomas Hobbes, *Leviathan,* chap. 14, ed. M. Oakeshott (New York: Collier Books, 1962), 103.

58. Plato, *Republic* 351d–e. See also Prov. 1:10–14; Judah Halevi *Kuzari* 2.48.

59. See Gough, *The Social Contract,* 110–13.

60. See Thomas Hobbes, *The Elements of Law* I, chap. 14, ed. J. C. A. Gaskin (Oxford: Oxford University Press, 1994), 77–81.

61. See Thomas Hobbes, *A Dialogue Between a Philosopher and a Student of the Common Laws of England,* ed. J. Cropsey (Chicago: University of Chicago Press, 1971), 73.

62. Plato, *Republic* 359c–360d.

63. Hobbes, *Leviathan,* ed. M. Oakeshott (New York: Collier Books, 1962), chap. 15, 113.

64. Ibid., chap. 17, 132.

65. *Babylonian Talmud:* Shabbat 88a re Exod. 19:17. See Novak, *Jewish Social Ethics,* 27–29.

66. Hobbes, chap. 14, 111.

67. See Ludwig Feuerbach, *The Essence of Christianity,* sec. 643–644, trans. George Eliot (Amherst, NY: Prometheus Books, 1989).

68. For the strengths and weaknesses of the covenantal political theology of the Puritans, see Perry Miller, *Errand Into the Wildnerness* (Cambridge, MA: Belknap Press, 1956), 60–68; J. D. Eusden, "Natural Law and Covenant Theology in New England: 1620–1670," *Natural Law Forum* 5 (1960), 1–30.

69. See, also, 1 Kings 19:11–12.

70. Charles Fried, *Contract As Promise* (Cambridge, MA: Harvard University Press, 1981), 8. See, also, Novak, *Covenantal Rights,* 3–8.

71. See *Babylonian Talmud:* Pesahim 68b and *Babylonian Talmud:* Nedarim 32a re Jer. 33:25.

72. See Gen. 18:17–25.

73. The rabbis saw the Epicureans as those whom the faithful should "know how to answer" (*Mishnah:* Avot 2.14). See also Maimonides, *Guide for the Perplexed* 3.17 re Jer. 5:12.

74. See Epicurus *Fragments* nos. 57–58, trans. C. Bailey in *The Stoic and Epicurean Philosophers,* ed. W. J. Oates (New York: Random House, 1940), 50. See also Cicero, *De Finibus* 1.18.

75. See *Targum Jonathan ben Uzziel:* Gen. 4:8; *Vayiqra Rabbah* 28.1; *Qohelet Rabbati* 1.4 re Eccl. 1:3.

76. See Machiavelli, *The Prince,* chapter 8.

77. The usual English translation, viz., "the fool says in his heart there is no God," follows the Vulgate: *Dicit insipiens in corde sua non est Deus.* Nevertheless, the Hebrew *naval* denotes willful moral fault, not just intellectual obtuseness (*in-sipiens*), see e.g., 1 Sam. 25:25. Indeed, a good case could be made that many contemporary public atheists object much more to the fact that the God of the Bible makes moral demands than the fact that the God of the Bible calls for human worship. See this author's review of Richard Dawkins's *The God Delusion* in *Azure,* 28 (2007), 123–30.

78. See Wittgenstein, *Tractatus Logico-Philosophicus,* 5.4731, 5.552, 5.6–62, 6.13, 6.3, 6.373; *Philosophical Investigations* I, nos. 242–46.

79. See *Babylonian Talmud:* Yevamot 6a re Lev. 19:3. For the universality of the duty to honor parents, see Saadiah Gaon, *Book of Beliefs and Opinions,* 3.2; Abraham ibn Ezra, *Commentary on the Torah:* Deut. 21:13; also, *Babylonian Talmud:* Kiddushin 31a.

80. See Kant, *Religion Within the Boundaries of Mere Reason,* trans. A. Wood and G. di Gioranni (Cambridge: Cambridge University Press, 1998), 4.2.2.1, note thereon, 165.

81. See David Novak, *The Image of the Non-Jew in Judaism* (New York: Edwin Mellen Press, 1983), 107–65.

82. But in John Locke's version of the social contract, even in the presocietal "state of nature" (which, by the way, is not a "state" in the sense of being a polity, but is a *status naturalis*) there is still enough natural community, theologically grounded, so that "no one ought to harm another . . . [f]or men being all the workmanship of one omnipotent, and infinitely wise Maker." *Second Treatise on Civil Government,* 2.6, 9, ed. C. B. Macpherson (Indianapolis: Hackett Publishing Co., 1980), 9. Cf. *Palestinian Talmud:* Nedarim 9.4/41c re Gen. 5:1 for an analogous "creationist" view.

83. *Mishnah:* Avot 3.2; also, *Babylonian Talmud:* Avodah Zarah 4a.

84. Aristotle, *Nicomachean Ethics* 8.1/1155a5.

85. *Babylonian Talmud:* Taanit 23a.

86. See Aristotle, *Nicomachean Ethics* 8.1/1155a20–29, 9.6/1167b1–4; *Politics* 4.9/1295b25.

87. Edmund Burke, *Appeal from the New to the Old Whigs,* ed. J. M. Robson (Indianapolis: Bobbs-Merrill, 1962), 96.

88. Cf. Ronald Dworkin, *Taking Rights Seriously* (Cambridge, MA: Harvard University Press, 1978), 198; also note 29 above.

Index

ABOUT THE AUTHOR

David Novak is the J. Richard and Dorothy Shiff Professor of Jewish Studies at the University of Toronto. A philosopher and theologian, he holds degrees from the University of Chicago and Georgetown University and a rabbinical diploma from the Jewish Theological Seminary of America. Novak's books include *Covenantal Rights: A Study in Jewish Political Theory*, *Talking with Christians: Musings of a Jewish Theologian*, and *The Sanctity of Human Life*.